ASIAN AMERICANS ON CAMPUS

While there are books on racism in universities, few examine the unique position of Asian American undergraduates. This new book captures the voices and experiences of Asian Americans navigating the currents of race, gender, and sexuality as factors in how youth construct relationships and identities. Interviews with 70 Asian Americans on an elite American campus show how students negotiate the sexualized racism of a large institution. The authors emphasize the students' resilience and their means of resistance for overcoming the impact of structural racism.

Rosalind S. Chou, Assistant Professor of Sociology at Georgia State University, is the author of *Asian American Sexual Politics* and co-author with Joe Feagin of *The Myth of the Model Minority*.

Kristen Lee, a second-generation Chinese American from Chicago, holds a degree in sociology from Duke University.

Simon Ho is an American-born Chinese from the Washington, DC area. He is currently an MD candidate at the University of Central Florida School of Medicine.

ASIAN AMERICANS ON CAMPUS

Racialized Space and White Power

Rosalind S. Chou, Kristen Lee, and Simon Ho

Routledge
Taylor & Francis Group
NEW YORK AND LONDON

First published 2016
by Routledge
711 Third Avenue, New York, NY 10017

and by Routledge
2 Park Square, Milton Park, Abingdon, Oxon, OX14 4RN

Routledge is an imprint of the Taylor & Francis Group, an informa business

© 2016 Taylor & Francis

The right of Rosalind S. Chou, Kristen Lee, and Simon Ho to be identified as authors of this work has been asserted by them in accordance with sections 77 and 78 of the Copyright, Designs and Patents Act 1988.

All rights reserved. No part of this book may be reprinted or reproduced or utilized in any form or by any electronic, mechanical, or other means, now known or hereafter invented, including photocopying and recording, or in any information storage or retrieval system, without permission in writing from the publishers.

Trademark notice: Product or corporate names may be trademarks or registered trademarks, and are used only for identification and explanation without intent to infringe.

Library of Congress Cataloging-in-Publication Data
A catalog record has been requested

ISBN: 978-1-61205-735-4 (hbk)
ISBN: 978-1-61205-736-1 (pbk)
ISBN: 978-1-315-67610-4 (ebk)

Typeset in Adobe Caslon
by Apex CoVantage, LLC

Printed and bound in the United States of America by Publishers Graphics, LLC on sustainably sourced paper.

Contents

PREFACE		VII
ACKNOWLEDGMENTS		IX
CHAPTER 1	INTRODUCTION: ASIAN AMERICANS ON CAMPUS	1
CHAPTER 2	WHITE SPACE, WHITE CAMPUS	19
CHAPTER 3	COLOR-BLIND DISCOURSE AND ASIAN AMERICAN SEXUAL POLITICS	41
CHAPTER 4	INTRARACIAL AND INTERRACIAL RELATIONSHIPS	61
CHAPTER 5	CONCLUSION: RESIGN OR RESIST? DISENGAGE OR ENGAGE?	95
REFERENCES		109
INDEX		113

PREFACE

I, Rosalind Chou, met Kristen Lee and Simon Ho after I had given a brief lecture at an Asian Student Association event in November 2010. The talk was centered on my research on Asian Americans, and I gave a general talk about racism and gendered racism that affected my interview participants in my two previous books, *The Myth of the Model Minority* and *Asian American Sexual Politics*. A small reception followed my talk, and as the food disappeared and the crowd dwindled, two students remained. They each had a list of questions about my presentation. I had anticipated an hour for my presentation and an hour for questions and mingling, and at that point I was concerned about the threat of a parking ticket. However, I could not leave our conversation. It became clear to me that Kristen and Simon were dissatisfied with their experiences on campus. Their highly ranked elite university was not quite the Promised Land they had anticipated. They were members of a working group on campus, trying to improve the campus climate after a few anti-Asian incidents had occurred. Their passion for scholarship was evident, and their desire to make a change for the better for Asian American students was the impetus of this book. They took it upon themselves to gather data, elevate the voices of the participants, and try to make sense of the Asian American experience on campus.

The persistence of the model minority myth, and the overrepresentation of Asian and Asian American students at colleges and universities across the United States, overshadows the discrimination and hostility these students face in these white spaces. Admission into historically prestigious institutions does not change the milieu or the racial order on campus. These campuses do not exist in a vacuum, and the racial hierarchy that exists in the United States is ever-present in the microcosms of college and universities. Most evident in my conversation with Simon and Kristen was that all they wanted from their university experience was to be treated as fully human, instead of foreign or as an outsider. This marginalization was sometimes overt but most often subtle. Being an outsider was evident in student leadership, powerful student organizations, the physical space of the university, and interactions with peers both on and off campus. The social scene is an important part of college students' lives, and race plays a role in peer groups, dating, and sex. The more we spoke and the more data were collected, it became evident how central race—specifically being Asian American—was to students' day-to-day interactions.

We hope our research and the analysis presented in this book will illuminate the experiences of Asian American college students. While each individual Asian American student has a unique experience, we hope to highlight that we all have a relationship to the preexisting social structure, with a racial social inertia that has been in place well before any of our time. We hope that by discussing the present campus climate of one particular institution we can further understand campus climates across the country. While time and location always matter, systemic racism, the white racial frame, and white habitus are essential pieces to white institutional spaces of higher education.

Acknowledgments

Simon would like to thank his faculty mentors, particularly Rosalind Chou, Linda Burton, Eduardo Bonilla-Silva, and Rebecca Bach, for their guidance and unending patience. Additionally, working with the participants has been a huge pleasure and has shown me the importance of asking ugly questions and speaking up. This research was supported in part by our Research Support Independent Study program and from the Janet Chiang program.

Kristen must begin by thanking her family. Her loud, opinionated Chinese American family may not always agree with her, but they have always listened with an open mind. Their love and support has been invaluable throughout this process. Furthermore, she wants to express her sincerest gratitude to faculty mentors Rosalind Chou, Eduardo Bonilla-Silva, and Kim Blankenship for their generosity of time and sociological imagination. It is a rare teacher whose lessons touch not only the minds but also the lives of their students. She is grateful for the time spent in their classrooms. She'd also like to recognize the student activists and faculty leaders who have continued to push their universities to do better for all students and who have personally challenged and inspired her. She hopes this book will offer insight to students and administrators alike on how colleges can become more proactive and less reactive to these important themes both in the classroom through education and in the construction of social spaces. Finally, she would like to thank the Asian American students who spoke up and participated in this study, and without whom this book would not have been possible.

Rosalind would like to thank her parents, Chuen Cheng and Li-Hsueh Chou, and two older sisters, Nina Sickler and Alice Chou. Special thanks to Kristen Lavelle, Jennifer Mueller, Glenn Bracey, Lorena Murga, Elyshia Aseltine, Daniel Delgado, Ruth Thompson-Miller, Christopher Chambers, Michelle Christian, Joe R. Feagin, Wendy Leo Moore, W. Alex McIntosh, Marian Eide, Stuart J. Hysom, Jane Sell, Ashley Currier, Eduardo Bonilla-Silva, Kerry L. Haynie, Paula D. McClain, Wendy Simonds, Ben Kail, Dawn Baunach, Heather Hale, Patty Jervey, Suzanne Uchneat, Emily Smith, Jason Payne, Tui Osborne, Dan Payne, all of my students and mentees, and especially two wonderful students I met during my time at Duke, Simon Ho and Kristen Lee.

1
INTRODUCTION
Asian Americans on Campus

I, Kristen Lee, grew up hearing this advice from my mother: "Just ignore them; they're idiots. High school is stupid like that. Wait until college." These words were spoken when I came home from high school upset over a peer singing "ching-chong" songs. They were repeated to me when I was angry about a friend telling me my straight-A performance was due to my "Asianness." Growing up in an upper-class white suburban environment I tried to blend in as much as possible, which was difficult considering I was one of a handful of Asian American students in my class. I began to count the days I would need to deal with high school students who pulled their eyelids to the sides to mock my Asian features and made insensitive jokes.

"Just ignore them; they're idiots. Just wait until college." It became a type of mantra for me to endure high school years. I would say it to myself repeatedly. It was a comforting thought. The way my mother talked about college, it sounded like a blank social check waiting for me to cash in. I did not need a "tiger mother"[1] to motivate me to study and apply for university; the promise of a space free of bullying and comments on my "Asianness" was enough to keep me after hours at the library studying for the SAT. To me, at the time, university meant freedom.

Looking back at my time at a top-ten university I have realized I was not prepared for the hidden university curriculum that is left out of admissions pamphlets. Coming to college, I was not prepared to deal with a white male student asking, "Why are there so many fucking Asians in the library?" I was not prepared to walk down the street and have a male shout out, "*Ni hao*, baby."[2] I was not prepared to have my friends shrug off these racialized experiences as me being "too sensitive" or "crazy." I had let my guard down with my mantra, with the myth that racism goes away as one climbs the ivory tower. I was not prepared for the pervasive, overt, and subtle racism that colored my university experiences. Drawn in by the laudable backgrounds of my peers and the prestige that comes with an elite university, I was not adequately prepared for the racism that was very much a part of university life.

When we first talked about writing this book, we realized there was a shortage of research that critically examines the lives of Asian American college students and does this through their own voices. While Asian American race scholarship has grown exponentially over these past few decades, much of the research lacks a critical race perspective, and in some cases, supports existing stereotypes that Asian Americans are high-achieving model minorities with few issues with racial discrimination.

Assumptions that Asian American students are largely high-achieving "model minorities" are inaccurate.[3] There are a number of factors that complicate generalizations: Asian Americans and Pacific Islanders (AAPIs) "are treated as though one percent of their enrollment can tell the story for the rest of the 99 percent of the college going population."[4] Also mythologized is that universities, including the most elite among them, together form a safe haven from ignorance and racial prejudice.[5] Contrary to the myth, the most prestigious American universities are not outside of the existing US racial structure; in fact, a normalized ideology and socialization process that "white is ideal" permeates every nook and cranny of this country including its most prestigious universities.[6]

In this book we challenge the one-dimensional notion that high enrollment of Asian Americans at colleges and universities protects them from racial discrimination. Such statistics are often used to further marginalize blacks and Latinos for their lower rates of college enrollment. Whites use Asian Americans to, in some ways, shame other groups of color, further cementing the existing racial hierarchy.[7] We also demonstrate the numerous ways that gendered racism affects Asian American students. Through an intersectional lens, we find that Asian Americans are influenced by racial constructions of gender and sexuality. In turn, these students either pull from or resist white standards of beauty and sexuality. We use qualitative interviews and respondent surveys to analyze the experiences of Asian American students at an elite university.[8] Our analysis addresses the following important questions: (1) How does the construction and regulation of gender, sexuality, and race of Asian Americans in white spaces support, or challenge, the racial status quo in the United States? (2) What toll does gendered racism take on Asian American students physically and mentally? (3) What is the Asian American experience at the university, and what can it tell us about race and racism today and about other historically white colleges and universities? Finally, we summarize our findings and look at the ways these Asian American students resist the gendered racism they face on campus.

Theoretical Overview

Systemic Racism and the White Racial Frame

We use a systemic racism approach to view racial oppression as a foundational and persisting underpinning of this society in the United States. From the beginning, powerful whites have designed and maintained the country's economic, political, and social institutions to benefit, disproportionately and substantially, their own racial group. For centuries, unjust impoverishment of Americans of color has been linked to unjust enrichment of whites, thereby creating a central racial hierarchy and status continuum in which whites are generally the dominant and privileged group.[9]

Since the earliest period of colonization, European Americans have sustained this hierarchical system of unjust material enrichment and unjust material impoverishment with legal institutions and a strong white racial *framing* of this society. These prestigious institutions have a history of gender and racial exclusion.[10] Understanding the historical context provides a foundation for the invisible, yet powerful, white norms and policies that shape and further reinforce the white racial frame on campus.

Understanding framing is essential to understanding how racism persists today and is disguised in institutions of higher education. Whites have combined within this pervasive white frame many racist stereotypes (the cognitive aspect), racist concepts (the deeper cognitive aspect), racist images (the visual aspect), racialized emotions (feelings), and inclinations to take discriminatory action.[11] The white racial frame is old, enduring, and oriented to assessing and relating to Americans of color in everyday situations. Operating with this racial frame firmly in mind, the dominant white group has used its power to place new non-European groups, such as Asian immigrants and their children, somewhere in the racial hierarchy that whites firmly control—that is, on a white-to-black continuum of status and privilege with whites at the highly privileged end, blacks at the unprivileged end, and other racial groups typically placed by whites somewhere in between.[12] This white racist framing is centuries old and continues to rationalize racism that has been systemic in this society. Situated centrally as institutions that pass along the central components of the white racial frame are historically white colleges and universities (HWCUs).

In opposition to the white racist framing and hegemonic framing of masculinity are three types of counter-frames: (1) a white crafted "liberty and justice" frame; (2) the anti-oppression counter-frames of Americans of color; and (3) the home-culture frames that Americans of color have drawn on in developing their counter-frames.[13] Asian Americans, collectively, have very few counter-frames from which to view alternative constructions of Asian American masculinity, femininity, or sexuality.[14] The externally imposed identity of "Asian American" represents many different cultures, which would provide a splintered or quilted "home-culture" frame with some overlap but a great deal of diversity of meanings and practices. Additionally, with more than half of Asians in the United States being newer immigrants, there are complications in identifying racist structure and oppression, which serves as another obstacle for developing strong "anti-oppression" counter-frames.[15]

Whether scholars choose to use "white racial framing," "white habitus," or racial "hegemony" to explain the persistence of racist thoughts, feelings, and practices, white supremacist ideology persists and comes in various forms embedded in institutions like US colleges and universities and in the psyches of whites students and students of color alike. Racist ideology is passed along subconsciously through "color-blind discourse" or subtly through racialized constructions of gender and sexuality.[16] Asian Americans students in this study have been socialized in a society where whiteness is normalized.

Model Minority

While Asian Americans make up only a small percentage of the nation's population, they are growing in numbers as well as socioeconomic status. Several demographic indicators suggest that Asian Americans are doing very well in America: They have a higher median income than any other racial group,[17] and they have the highest rates of achieving a college degree compared to other racial groups.[18] Asian American overrepresentation in upper-tier American universities is often used as proof that racial minorities can be successful if they just work hard enough and that racism is not a barrier.[19] While they comprise only 5 percent of the total population of the United States, Asian Americans make up to 30 percent of the student population in some elite universities. Following the Immigration Act of 1965, the United States has seen a huge increase in the number of foreign-born Asian Americans, and the median income of Asian Americans has surpassed that of white non-Hispanic Americans within the last several decades. It is from such achievements that Asian Americans have often been labeled the "model minority."[20]

However, the statistics cited on Asian Americans as a demographic only draw attention to one side of a bimodal population. Although statistics show Asian Americans have made strides in educational and economic achievement, on the whole they suffer from a poverty rate higher than that of non-Hispanic whites, and more Asian Americans than whites have not finished high school.[21] These differences are evidence of an Asian American dichotomy—two different Asian Americas that are often lumped together despite their drastically different histories.

The perceptions of Asian Americans as the "model minority" are mainly a result of the accomplishments of successful East Asians who immigrated to the United States in the later twentieth century.[22] "[They] tend to be college-educated, have middle-class occupations, and live outside of the inner-city Chinatowns."[23] However, these "accomplishments" do not protect Asian Americans from negative stereotyping or racial discrimination.[24] In fact, the white-crafted "model minority" stereotype creates cleavages in creating multiracial coalitions as Asian Americans are stereotyped as "near white."[25] Additionally, what is often downplayed is the existence of the "FOB" (Fresh Off the Boat) population, who are "poorly educated and deficient in English, live in Chinatowns, and ply the low-wage service trades or sweatshop manufacturing plants typical of inner cities."[26] The bifurcation of the Asian American population is one not recognized by the mainstream American public, and not well represented by the mainstream media. Thus, in the white racial frame, there is the one-dimensional view that Asian American college students have "made it" or are living the "American Dream." In our intersectional analysis, we demonstrate that their experiences are more varied and complex.

Twenty-First-Century Racism: Roots of Color-blindness

The overt Jim Crow racism that ruled through segregation, derogatory language, and violence has in many ways been replaced by the subtleties of contemporary racism.[27] Today, racism still operates as a system based on an ideology of inferiority that allocates societal resources by racial hierarchy.[28] However, the "new" racism is more covert, more likely to dance around inferiority and inequality in the hidden language of "differences." Though the literature has chronicled various forms of this post–Civil Rights era racism, in the context of this book we focus on what Eduardo Bonilla-Silva refers to as *color-blind racism*. A type of "racism without racists," color-blind racism is a racial ideology that allows whites to defend their racial interests while maintaining invisibility of whiteness and white privilege. Color-blindness refuses to examine racism within a social and historical context. It reduces race problems to matters of isolated individual prejudice and negates the existence of a larger socioeconomic racial structure with real economic, social, and political consequences for people of color.²⁹ Common elements of color-blind racism are: (1) to discuss racial matters in the abstract, (2) to attribute racially inferior standings in education and economy to cultural differences over biological explanations, (3) to frame racial residential and school segregation as "natural," and (4) to claim discrimination as a thing of the past (Bonilla-Silva 2002). To the color-blind, the problem is never race or racism. Through various denial strategies, color-blind racism obfuscates the problem of racial inequality, thus making it difficult to dismantle the white ruling class.

Color-blind Racism

In *Racism without Racists: Color-Blind Racism and the Persistence of Racial Inequality in the United States*, Eduardo Bonilla-Silva conceptualizes four discursive frames used to explain racial incidents and inequalities as anything but racism.³⁰ The first frame in Bonilla-Silva's theory is *abstract liberalism*. This form of liberalism is a way for whites to invoke ideas of "equality," "fairness," and "meritocracy."³¹ The implication of abstract liberalism is that in order to be successful, minorities must work hard, like whites, while ignoring the long history of institutional discrimination and the perpetual unleveled playing field. By touting Asian Americans as the "model minority," whites have found their "paragon" to legitimize color-blind racist rhetoric. Whites depend and rely on the model minority construction to minimize and disguise white supremacy. If whites can claim that Asian Americans are "outwhiting the whites" then it shifts the blame from white imposed systemic racism to individual responsibility for racial inequality.

Color-blind racism principally operates through the expression of conversations, media, and other forms of communication. There are numerous parts to communicating color-blind racism, but for the purpose of this book we highlight three of its discursive practices: (1) the use of certain semantics to express racial views, (2) the almost complete incoherence when it comes to certain issues of race, and (3) the minimization of concerns about racial inequality.³²

To adapt to the shift from Jim Crow racism to post-Civil Rights era realities where openly racist statements were no longer socially acceptable, color-blind discourse opted for specific language to express racial views. For example, one might couch a racist statement by emphasizing that it is not a racist comment. One might also use descriptors that are tacitly racialized, such as describing a neighborhood as "ghetto" when he or she means to say it is a minority community. The incoherence regarding certain issues of race is sometimes characterised by long pauses, and "I don't know" statements when speaking on themes of race make difficult the identification and resolution of racist incidents. The minimization of concerns about racial inequality are fostered in color-blind racism not only by denying racial structure but also by silencing those who raise the issue. For example, individuals might call Asian Americans outraged by racial discrimination "too sensitive" or "overreacting," in essence minimizing racism as an emotional problem. Embedded in the subtleties of talk, color-blind discourse may appear benign compared to the system of fear and violence that Jim Crow racism employed. However, color-blind discourse could be more powerful for its tacit hegemony, moving through the minds of the majority and minority alike.[33]

White Habitus

This process of learning that whiteness is the standard, or ideal, is explained by Eduardo Bonilla-Silva, Carla Goar, and David Embrick.[34] These scholars assert that whiteness is normalized by *white habitus*, a "racialized uninterrupted socialization process that conditions and creates whites' racial tastes, perceptions, feelings, and emotions and their views on racial matters." Color-blind racism is a product of the white habitus because whites are racially segregated from people of color. However, the power of white habitus to shape views on race and racial matters can invade the spaces of people of color. The ideology produced from white habitus—color-blind racism—is adopted by people of color as they are both segregated by whites and regularly operate in largely white spaces, like the elite university.

White habitus, or the socialization process of adopting dominant, oppressive ideology, is described somewhat differently in gender and sexuality scholarship. Instead of white habitus, *hegemonic masculinity* is used to describe the powerful ideology of domination and how the ideas become normalized.[35] Hegemonic masculinity is typically associated with white, middle-/upper-class, straight men. This is the ideal, normal man—all others are inferior. Application of white habitus must include an intersectional approach, and in this case we include hegemonic masculinity. Additionally, white habitus is not just a socialization process for whites. While Bonilla-Silva and Embrick focus on this process, which "creates and conditions [white] views, cognitions, and even sense of beauty,"[36] we argue that white habitus permeates beyond the borders of segregated white spaces and that the meanings can be adopted by people of color—in this case, by Asian Americans. Scholars have argued that white habitus can be reproduced in a multiracial setting and employed by people of color.[37] We argue that an intersectional approach to color-blind racism is necessary. White habitus socializes and shapes Asian American students at colleges and universities through intersecting domains of power and through exclusion in largely white spaces.

Hegemonic Masculinity and Femininity

Navigating gender structure generally involves the theory of hegemonic sexualities—the idea that certain masculinities and femininities exist that provide cultural and social capital and are culturally and socially superior to other subordinated masculinities and femininities.[38] These masculinities and femininities are resoundingly white, upper-class, and straight, while subordinate sexualities are poor, colored, and nonheterosexual. This theory of a hierarchy of physical sexualities complements Bonilla-Silva's tri-racial model, in which he suggests the formation of a three-tiered hierarchy where US inhabitants gain social capital as a result of their skin color.[39] Whites gain the most benefit, followed by lighter-skinned minorities like some Asians and some Latinos, while blacks and darker-skinned racial minorities suffer the most.

The hierarchy of hegemonic sexualities complements the idea of multiple romantic capitals. While phenotypic capital is most obviously implied in the structure of hegemonic sexuality, other types of capital have their place in hegemonic sexuality. For example, language capital carries weight in attraction—different accents and languages have respective disparate values. For example, whereas European accents, particularly British accents, have been romanticized, Asian accents have been discounted. Ideological framing carries romantic weight as well, as traditional gender role frames have been appreciated while more progressive framing has been depreciated. This is clear even in R.W. Connell's writing about "emphasized" femininity as opposed to "hegemonic" femininity. In this framework, to gain the most structural advantage women must always recognize their position subordinate to men. This is also the case for racial minorities who do not question the racial status quo; they generally receive more privilege than those who do.

Individuals with more phenotypic capital are awarded certain privileges and mobility in society, especially in places that institutionally promote white centricity. While the historically white elite university is a multiracial and ethnically diverse space, it has been shown to reproduce white supremacy.[40] Previous studies affirm that Asian Americans are subject to this white institutional pressure and are adversely affected by it, though many Asian students integrate and perpetrate this system.[41] For example, Chou and colleagues in previous analysis of the data found that while some resist white centrality and others are resigned to it, all self-identifying Asian students required some level of emotional management to function in a space that subordinates Asian sexuality and racial identity.[42]

Intersectionality and Interracial Relationships

In *Black Sexual Politics*, Patricia Hill Collins suggests that race and gender have overlapping and combinatory effects, such that different combinations of gender and race are constructed differently.[43] The perspective, termed *intersectionality*, has been used to explain the different patterns that exist in Asian American male and female sexuality.[44] Historically, Asian men and women have been socially constructed with different controlling images.[45] Early Asian sojourners were mostly men involved in manual labor, and their images were socially constructed similar to those of black men: aggressive and hypersexual, especially toward white women. As immigration grew and Asian men looked to other forms of domestic labor for jobs, they become constructed as castrated and weak-willed. Later, as Asian women arrived in large numbers, they became exotified as either dangerous "dragon ladies" or delicate "china dolls." Although these images seem different, the creation of each emphasized the white man's virility.[46] These omnipresent controlling images in the media exacerbate the "oriental fetishism" Asian and Asian American women face.[47] Controlling images affecting both Asian American men and women exist "to define the white man's virility and the white man's superiority."[48] At the core of this imaging is the strength of the white habitus and hegemonic masculinity.[49] The necessity to define white male virility and superiority through demeaning images of Asian Americans is essential in retaining the existing racial structure.

Drawing on these historical images, we suggest here that intersectionality explains disparate attitudes and approaches toward interracial romance among Asian American men and women. For example, the pattern of reverse out-marriage (where Asian men out-marry less than women) can be explained through the almost universal "castration" of Asian American men since the 1960s, whereas Asian women have been subjected to more sexualized constructions.[50] This is counter to more current constructions of other men of color (particularly blacks and Latinos), who have been relatively oversexualized.[51]

Intersectionality entails different positions for people of color on a hegemonic sexuality hierarchy. This means that across races, people of color gain different levels of capital based on their gender, and vice versa. Collins recognizes how this contributes to black gender disparity in different economic sectors: For example, black men are eschewed from the service sector of work due to being constructed as overly masculine and dangerous.[52] In other words, black men lack a "comfort" capital that black women have relatively more of. In *Asian American Sexual Politics*, Chou suggests that Asians, and particularly Asian women, have been awarded certain social capital based on their race/gender characteristics.[53]

People of color are placed in different places on a hegemonic sexuality scale. This structure is similar to Bonilla-Silva's tri-racial model. Racial minorities closer to whites who gain honorary white status and privilege are more likely to navigate the white racial frame and white supremacist ideologies. In prior research, my colleagues and I have found that Asian Americans, particularly East Asians in elite universities, use color-blind ideology and white racial framing in their narratives, as well as showing high levels of racial double consciousness.

We suggest that having honorary white privileges (especially those afforded by hegemonic sexualities) correlates with white racial framing and results in racial double consciousness.

Institutional Racism and White Spaces

Elites occupy a powerful role in shaping and perpetuating the discourse that reproduces racism.[54] White power and privilege no longer rule through outright violence and intimidation. Instead, social practices enabled by institutional structure maintain racial hierarchy. As a formative educational institution, the university is particularly positioned to perpetuate white ideologies through its discursive academic and social practices.[55] Wendy Moore in *Reproducing Racism* details how law schools simultaneously assert themselves as neutral institutions but indoctrinate in their students an understanding of economic, political, and social interactions founded on white hegemonic ideologies.[56] Joe Feagin draws our attention to the university social climate, riddled with racial stereotyping and hostility toward students of color.[57] Failing to investigate the racial character of these predominately white educational institutions, which Bonilla-Silva terms *historically white colleges and universities* (HWCUs), keeps us from addressing the racial inequality such institutions reproduce.[58]

Several scholars have noted that many studies fail to connect Asian American health problems with the "pressures of everyday racism."[59] Asian American females aged fifteen to twenty-four have the highest suicide rate of all the racial groups, and they have reported feeling as if they faced greater expectations and pressures to achieve, especially educationally, than their peers.[60] Furthermore, the distribution of space in institutions of higher learning is highly racialized to facilitate white supremacy, taxing students of color who navigate such spaces both emotionally and physically. The purpose of this research is to describe the racialized experiences with white habitus and white spaces that Asian Americans must negotiate at the university level.[61]

Our Asian American Sample

Though there is much work to be done in understanding the experiences of all Asian Americans and Pacific Islanders, we focus here primarily on the experiences of East Asian American undergraduates. This project involved two qualitative research instruments rolled out in two phases from 2011 to 2012.

In the initial stage, semistructured face-to-face interviews were conducted with fourteen Asian American undergraduates at an elite university hereafter referred to as Elite University. We recruited participants through purposive sampling in an attempt to gain a diverse demographic sampling and reflect a broad set of experiences.[62] Our respondents self-identified as Chinese (1 female, 2 males), Taiwanese (2 females, 1 male), Korean (2 females, 3 males), Indian (1 female), Hapa ("hapa" denotes half Japanese; this particular respondent self-identified as hapa, a mix of Japanese and Irish descent) (1 male), and Pacific Islander (1 female). The geographical distribution was varied, with those surveyed residing on the West Coast (3), North East (3), Deep South (2), South Atlantic (3), Midwest (1), and Pacific West (1); the remaining subject is a first-generation immigrant who self-identified as an international student. Of the interviewees, thirteen were undergraduate students and one was a graduate student. Ages ranged from eighteen to twenty-four years. Interviews consisted of a number of open-ended questions on family experiences, body image and media influences, hook-ups/dating/marriage, the university social scene, and the presence of counter-narratives. On average, interviews lasted two hours and were recorded and transcribed.

The second mode of inquiry utilized an open-ended qualitative online questionnaire based on the semistructured interview questions to collect data from forty-seven additional Asian American undergraduates from Elite University, for a total of sixty-one respondents. Survey participants were recruited via flyers, e-mails to Asian American organizations, and the university's social science participant data base. The survey collected demographic information on the respondents' age, gender, sexuality, ethnicity, education level, number of relationships, and citizenship status. It also included a number of open-ended questions on familial expectations, social relationships, and racialized experiences growing up and at university. Of our forty-seven questionnaire participants, twenty-seven were female, and twenty were male. Respondents self-identified as Chinese (22), Asian (6), Asian

American (8), Indian (2), Korean (3), Taiwanese (3), Mixed Japanese (1), and Vietnamese (2). Respondents self-identified their sexuality as straight (40), bi-sexual (3), gay (1), asexual (1), and bi-curious (1), with one nonrespondent. Ages ranged from eighteen to twenty-two years. Respondents are identified in this book via pseudonym.[63]

The results of both the interview and survey data were examined through narrative analysis and coding techniques.[64] Narrative analysis takes as its starting point the belief that we understand our experiences and ourselves by telling stories. These can be as specific as accounts of particular events, or as broad as an entire life story. Our task during narrative analysis was to understand participant stories, examining not only their content but also their structure. Although individuals are sharing these narratives, other elements of social life affect their experiences. Their storytelling will incorporate larger ideologies of placement in social structure, media discourse, and cultural values. As Asian American researchers, we also embraced reflexivity throughout the research process. This process allowed the researchers to consider how our own experiences, assumptions, and context could color the interpretation of participant narratives. As we gathered and analyzed our data systematically, we coded and recoded our field notes into categories emerging during the process. This encouraged us to reflect critically on how we analyzed and assembled knowledge. Through this analysis, the data in this book offers rare insight into the racialized experiences of Asian American undergraduates.

Conclusion and Overview

Our central aim in this book is to explore the diversity of experiences of Asian American students at an elite university and find the ways in which they may speak more broadly to the experiences of Asian Americans on college campuses across the United States. In the following chapters we examine signifcant questions about the construction and regulation of gender, sexuality, and race of Asian Americans on historically white college and university campuses. We are especially interested in learning if these white spaces support, or challenge, the racial status quo and if Asian Americans are affected physically and mentally. By examining these questions we want to determine if there are racial themes that emerge for Asian Americans at the university and what that can tell us about race and racism today and about other historically white colleges and universities. Additionally, we look at the ways these Asian American students resist gendered racism.

In Chapter 2 we introduce our key concepts. With the use of respondent narratives, we detail how Asian American masculinity and femininity are constructed and how they operate in a racial hierarchy. These accounts illuminate the gendered and sexualized racism faced by Asian Americans. We argue that this gendering and sexualizing process plays a specific role in maintaining the racial status quo. Our respondents detail ways in which they were pressured or influenced to meet certain gendered racialized or sexualized expectations. Most notably, both male and female respondents speak positively about their bodies when they seem *less* Asian and closer to "white" features. There are notable differences in the experiences of men and women.

In Chapter 3 we examine the way Asian Americans describe social settings, and the role of color-blind discourse. We explore the way Asian Americans face the emotional challenges of resisting and resigning to sexualized and everyday racism. We analyze narratives that discuss how intersected racial and gender identity affects self-image and self-esteem. The women discuss psychological and emotional well-being relative to racial and gender identities. We also focus on the components of white space at an elite university and how white space promotes and perpetuates gendered and racialized stereotypes of Asian Americans. Gender socialization positions Asian Americans on the lower rungs of an intersected racial hierarchy and thus influences "racial romantic taste."

In Chapter 4 our data reveals how sexual and romantic relationships are formed, and we examine the dynamics of Asian American intraracial and interracial relationships. Respondents balance messages from their families and external racialized forces. There is a hierarchy of partners based on race, ethnicity, class, and gender. Respondents discuss relationship hardship and success. The male respondents share experiences that highlight how "racial castration" occurs in the socialization of Asian American men. Asian American women are met with an exotification and Orientalization as sexual bodies but are also awarded a unique empowerment that is not as available to their male counterparts.

In Chapter 5 we summarize our findings and discuss their implications, drawing larger conclusions about how race and gender operate in the lives of Asian Americans on college campuses. We also address the areas in need of further research from the implications that have arisen from our analysis. We conclude by addressing the broader implications of our research for understanding US society and for policies that may help lift the weight of everyday racism and sexism.

Notes

1. This term was made famous by author Amy Chua, stereotyping the Asian and Asian American mother as strict or demanding, pushing her children to high levels of achievement, using methods regarded as typical of childrearing in China and other parts of East Asia.
2. *Ni hao* is Mandarin Chinese that translates to "hello."
3. Rosalind S. Chou and Joe R. Feagin, *The Myth of the Model Minority: Asian Americans Facing Racism* (Boulder, CO: Paradigm, 2014); Robert T. Teranishi, *Asians in the Ivory Tower: Dilemmas of Racial Inequality in American Higher Education* (New York: Teachers College Press, 2010).
4. Teranishi, *Asians in the Ivory Tower*, 105.
5. Chou and Feagin, *The Myth of the Model Minority*; Teranishi, *Asians in the Ivory Tower*; Mia Tuan, *Forever Foreigners or Honorary Whites? The Asian Ethic Experience* (New Brunswick, NJ: Rutgers University Press, 2003).
6. Joe R. Feagin, *Racist America: Roots, Current Realities, and Future Reparations* (New York: Routledge, 2014).
7. Chou and Feagin, *The Myth of the Model Minority*.
8. We define "elite university" as ranked in the top fifty, first tier of *US News and World Report* college rankings.
9. Feagin, *Racist America*.
10. Wendy Moore, *Reproducing Racism* (Lanham, MD: Rowman and Littlefield, 2008).
11. Joe R. Feagin, *The White Racial Frame: Centuries of Racial Framing and Counter-Framing* (New York: Routledge, 2009).
12. Chou and Feagin, *The Myth of the Model Minority*.
13. Feagin, *The White Racial Frame*.
14. Rosalind S. Chou, *Asian American Sexual Politics: The Construction of Race, Gender, and Sexuality* (Lanham, MD: Rowman and Littlefield, 2012).
15. Ibid.
16. Ibid.
17. US Census, 2006.
18. Ibid.
19. Chou and Feagin, *The Myth of the Model Minority*; Teranishi, *Asians in the Ivory Tower*.
20. Frank Wu, *Yellow: Race in America beyond Black and White* (New Haven, CT: Yale University Press, 2003).
21. US Census Bureau, 2004, "American Community Survey," Selected Population Profiles, S0201.
22. Harry R.L. Kitano, *Asian Americans: Emerging Minorities* (New York: Prentice Hall, 2004); Teranishi, *Asians in the Ivory Tower*.
23. Teranishi, *Asians in the Ivory Tower*, 51–52.
24. Chou and Feagin, *The Myth of the Model Minority*.

25. Ibid.
26. Teranishi, *Asians in the Ivory Tower*, 53.
27. Eduardo Bonilla-Silva, "The Linguistics of Color Blind Racism: How to Talk Nasty about Blacks without Sounding 'Racist'" *Critical Sociology* 28, no. 1 (2002): 41–64.
28. Eduardo Bonilla-Silva, "Rethinking Racism: Toward a Structural Interpretation," *American Sociological Review* 62, no. 3 (June 1997): 465–480.
29. Vijay Prashad, "Genteel Racism," *Amerasia Journal* 26, no. 3 (2001): 27–31.
30. Bonilla-Silva, "The Linguistics of Color Blind Racism."
31. Ibid.
32. Ibid.
33. Teun van Dijk, "New(s) Racism: A Discourse Analytical Approach," in Simon Cottle (ed.), *Ethnic Minorities and the Media*, 33–49 (Milton Keynes, UK: Open University Press, 2000).
34. Eduardo Bonilla-Silva, Carla Goar, and David G. Embrick, "When Whites Flock Together: The Social Psychology of White Habitus," *Critical Sociology* 32, nos. 2–3 (2007): 229–253; Eduardo Bonilla-Silva and David G. Embrick, "'Every Place Has a Ghetto . . .': The Significance of Whites' Social and Residential Segregation," *Journal of Symbolic Interaction* 30, no. 3 (2007): 323–346.
35. R.W. Connell and James Messerschmidt, "Hegemonic Masculinity: Rethinking the Concept," *Gender and Society* 19, no. 6 (2005): 845–854.
36. Bonilla-Silva and Embrick, "Every Place Has a Ghetto," 340.
37. Meghan Burke, "Discursive Fault Lines: Reproducing White Habitus in a Racially Diverse Community," *Critical Sociology* (2012): 645–668.
38. Connell and Messerschmidt, "Hegemonic Masculinity: Rethinking the Concept."
39. Eduardo Bonilla-Silva, "From Bi-racial to Tri-racial: Towards a New System of Racial Stratification in the USA," *Ethnic and Racial Studies* 27, no. 6 (2004).
40. Moore, *Reproducing Racism*.
41. See, for example, Rosalind S. Chou, Kristen Lee, and Simon Ho, "The White Habitus and Hegemonic Masculinity at the Elite Southern University: Asian Americans and the Need for Intersectional Analysis," *Sociation Today* 10, no. 2 (2012).
42. Ibid.
43. Patricia Hill Collins, *Black Sexual Politics* (New York: Routledge, 2004).
44. Chou and Feagin, *The Myth of the Model Minority*.
45. Yen Le Espiritu, *Asian American Women and Men: Labor, Laws, and Love* (Lanham, MD: Rowman and Littlefield, 2008).
46. Elaine Kim, "'Such Opposite Creatures': Men and Women in Asian American Literature," *Michigan Quarterly Review* 29 (1990): 70.
47. Sheridan Prasso, *The Asian Mystique: Dragon Ladies, Geisha Girls, and Our Fantasies of the Exotic Orient* (Cambridge, MA: Public Affairs, 2006).
48. Kim, "'Such Opposite Creatures.'"
49. Rosalind S. Chou, *Asian American Sexual Politics: The Construction of Race, Gender, and Sexuality* (Lanham, MD: Rowman and Littlefield, 2012).
50. David Eng, *Racial Castration: Managing Masculinity in Asian America (Perverse Modernities)* (Durham, NC: Duke University Press, 2001).
51. Kim, "'Such Opposite Creatures.'"
52. Collins, *Black Sexual Politics*.
53. Chou, *Asian American Sexual Politics*.
54. Van Dijk, "New(s) Racism: A Discourse Analytical Approach."
55. Moore, *Reproducing Racism*.
56. Ibid.
57. Joe R. Feagin, "The Continuing Significance of Racism: US Colleges and Universities," *American Council on Education, Office of Minorities in Higher Education* 1, no. 4 (2002): 1–54.

58. Eduardo Bonilla-Silva, "The Invisible Weight of Whiteness: The Racial Grammar of Everyday Life in Contemporary America," *Ethnic and Racial Studies* 35, no. 2 (2012): 183–185.
59. Mitchell J. Chang, "Battle Hymn of the Model Minority Myth," *Amerasia Journal* 37, no. 2 (2011): 137–143; Chou and Feagin, *Myth of the Model Minority*.
60. The Office of Minority Health, 2012, Health Status of Asian American and Pacific Islander Women, http://minorityhealth.hhs.gov.
61. Moore, *Reproducing Racism*.
62. Norman K. Denzin and Yvonna S. Lincoln (eds.) *The Sage Handbook of Qualitative Research*. Third edition. (Thousand Oaks, CA: Sage Publications, 2005).
63. We have lightly edited the interview quotes for grammar, stutter words ("you know"), and clarity. Pseudonyms are given to all respondents to conceal their identity, and some details have been omitted or disguised in the quotes from interviews to increase the anonymity of participants.
64. Michael Burawoy, 1998, "The Extended Case Method," in *Ethnography Unbound*, edited by M. Burawoy, A. Burton, A.A. Ferguson, K.J. Fox, J. Gamson, N. Gartrell, L. Hurst, C. Kurzman, L. Salzinger, J. Schiffman, and S. Ui (Berkeley: University of California Press, 1991), 271–287; "The Extended Case Method," *Sociological Theory* 16, no. 1: 4–33; Anselm L. Strauss, *Qualitative Analysis for Social Scientists* (New York: Cambridge University Press, 1987).

2
WHITE SPACE, WHITE CAMPUS

Introduction

In January 2014, the chancellor of the University of Illinois–Urbana Champagne, Phyllis Wise, an Asian American, did not grant her students a snow day. While snow and ice were disrupting classes on campuses across the country that winter, most notable was the social media reaction to Chancellor Wise. The online reactions of students to the chancellor turned into sexist and racist attacks. With the Twitter handle #fuckphyllis, students tweeted "Communist China no stop by cold," "Asians and women aren't responsible for their actions," and "Phyllis Wise is the Kim Jong Un of chancellors." At a nearby campus, University of Wisconsin–Lacrosse, white chancellor Joe Gow was not met with the same attacks. In fact, students used humor and even made reference to Star Wars character Luke Skywalker, valiantly and stoically leading the campus on through the storm.[1] The drastic difference in the reactions of these students demonstrates the power of white institutional space.

Wise holds the most powerful position at the flagship state university in Illinois, and was born in the United States. Yet the Twitter attacks that mocked her with broken English and utilized an age-old stereotype of Asian women as "heartless dragon ladies" by comparing her to North Korean dictator Kim Jong Un. As President Barack Obama has shown, holding leadership in the highest positions in the United States does not protect people of color from racist stereotyping. White institutional space trumps individual effort, maintaining the racial status quo. Throughout Obama's presidency (and during his campaigns) he has been a target of racist attacks that are also often gendered and sexualized—including stereotyping associated with the myth of the "dangerous black man."

As we discussed in Chapter 1, it is mythologized that the university environment is a safe haven from ignorance and racial prejudice. In fact, college campuses are part of society, and racism is foundational to the United States.[2] Our most prestigious universities are not outside of the existing US racial structure, where a normalized ideology and socialization process that promotes the notion that "white is ideal" permeates every nook and cranny of this country.[3]

White Insitutional Space, White Habitus

Historically white colleges and universities (HWCUs) have been utilized for centuries as institutions to enrich students through their curriculum, providing them with the necessary knowledge and skills to be "productive members of society." They also serve to socialize students to a distinct campus climate. These institutions, formerly exclusively white—and many still overwhelmingly so—normalize a certain kind of personhood.[4] While HWCUs were legally racially segregated, they became what Wendy Moore refers to as "white institutionalized spaces" where there is a process of learning that "whiteness is right." Eduardo Bonilla-Silva, Carla Goar, and David Embrick assert that whiteness is normalized by "white habitus," which they define as a "racialized uninterrupted socialization process that conditions and creates whites' racial tastes, perceptions, feelings, and emotions and their views on racial matters."[5] The socialization process of whites shapes their racial tastes, perceptions, and feelings. Elites occupy a powerful role in shaping and perpetuating the discourse that reproduces racism.[6] White power and privilege no longer rule through outright violence and intimidation; instead, social practices enabled by institutional structure maintain racial hierarchy. As a formative educational institution, the university is particularly positioned to perpetuate white ideologies through its discursive academic and social practices.[7] We argue that an elite campus can also have this effect on people of color in three additional ways: (1) when it allows white peers to racially stereotype other students, (2) as demonstrated through staff and student use of color-blind discourse, and (3) in how students describe their romantic tastes and interests.

Feagin's definition of "white racial framing" accounts for people of color who adopt these white normalized ideologies.[8] Chou and Feagin contend that Asian Americans, at times, also see the world through a white racial frame and thus internalize racist messaging and negative stereotyping of other people of color.[9] Gender and sexuality scholarship uses terms like *hegemonic masculinity* to discuss the powerful ideology of domination and how ideas become normalized.[10] Hegemonic masculinity is racialized, as men of color are "marginalized masculinities" and are stereotyped as less than ideal compared to white men.[11] While Bonilla-Silva and Embrick focus on this process, which "creates and conditions [white] views, cognitions, and even sense of beauty" in segregated white spaces, we argue that "white habitus" permeates beyond the borders of those all-white spaces and is tacitly present throughout campuses in the United States.[12] The meanings derived from these spaces can be adopted by people of color—in this case, by Asian Americans. Here, we assert that Asian American students are socialized in the white habitus known as an elite university.

Wendy Moore specifically addresses campus climate at elite law schools, but white institutionalized space describes all HWCUs. Assumptions that Asian American students are largely high-achieving "model minorities" are inaccurate.[13] Through such a generalization, "AAPIs are treated as though one percent of their enrollment can tell the story for the rest of the 99 percent of the college going population."[14] Also mythologized is that the university is a safe haven from ignorance and racial prejudice; however, Asian Americans are not free of racism on campus.[15]

The components of white institutional space are: (1) racist exclusion of people of color from access to and from positions of power, (2) development of the white racial frame in the context that organizes institutional logic, (3) historical development of a curriculum based upon the white racial frame, and (4) assertion of curriculum as a neutral, impartial body of doctrine unconnected to power.[16] Through this process, students of all races are socialized into the racial order and, perhaps, fail to question the racial status quo. This places colleges and universities at the core of the social structure of racial domination.

More than Race—Intersections of Gender and Sexuality

This socialization is not only a racialized process but also an intersectional one that shapes racial, gendered, and sexualized thoughts, feelings, and attitudes. Additionally, the white habitus enveloping Asian American students can be strengthened by exclusion from white spaces on campus. David Eng argues that racial analysis of Asian Americans is inadequate without the consideration of how their sexuality has been constructed.[17] Eng's point becomes clearly apparent with our respondent narratives. Asian American men face a particular placement on a gendered hierarchy and deal with battles against normalized constructions of masculinity that operate differently than their Latino or African American male counterparts.[18] Asian Americans have specific racial stereotypes imposed upon them by others, but that identity does not stand alone. Race intersects gender and sexuality in a particular way. Racial stereotypes can and do change over time, but they continue to exist to maintain the racial status quo. The stereotyping of early male Chinese immigrants was very similar to past and current constructions of African American men as hypersexual, aggressive, and dangerous.[19] However, over time, these stereotypes of Asian American men changed, and now they are constructed as hyposexual, impotent, and weak.[20]

Western film and literature constructs Asian women in a dichotomous fashion, as either a cunning "dragon lady" or a servile "lotus blossom."[21] Both of these constructions eroticize Asian women.[22] These omnipresent controlling images in the media exacerbate the "oriental fetishism" Asian and Asian American women face.[23] Controlling images affecting both Asian American men and women exist "to define the white man's virility and the white man's superiority."[24] At the core of this imaging is the strength of white habitus and hegemonic masculinity.[25] The necessity to define white male virility and superiority through demeaning images of Asian Americans is essential in retaining the existing racial structure.

As mentioned in the previous chapter, Asian Americans comprise only 5 percent of the total population of the United States but make up to 30 percent of the student population in some elite universities, which reinforces the stereotype that Asian Americans are "model minorities" and excel in the classroom. These stereotypes persist and even some prominent Asian Americans perpetuate this idea. In 2011 Amy Chua, a professor at Yale Law School, published a book describing the "parenting methods used by Chinese parents."[26] *The Battle Hymn of the Tiger Mother*, after being discussed in a *Wall Street Journal* article entitled "Why Chinese Mothers Are Superior," sparked national debate and even an Internet meme based on the "tiger mother." Though Chua did offer a disclaimer that "Chinese mothers" did not refer to all Chinese mothers, her depiction of parenting by Asian parents draws attention to how "abnormal" or "different" it is from "American" or "Western" parenting. Chua stigmatizes Asian American students and what she claims is their familial upbringing.

White Space, White Campus, and the Hidden Curriculum

Often uninterrogated is the physical space and layout in educational settings. Within the physical structure and design of the campus we can find racial signifiers of power.[27] These underlying messages within the physical space are what Eric Margolis calls the "hidden curriculum."[28] While Moore was specifically looking at elite law schools, our respondents were all enrolled at an elite university, ranked as a top institution for the past several decades. On this campus, the white Greek system *is* the center of campus. While other colleges and universities in the United States require fraternities and sororities to be off campus, or on the fringes, the students at this university who are members of those Greek organizations get the prime real estate at the university, with their housing put on display as the centerpiece. This Greek system is also the epicenter for student social life, further cementing a racialized order on campus, yet as "hidden curriculum."

Chou and Feagin contend that many Asian American college students feel like racial outsiders on college campuses across the country.[29] One respondent, Indira, well described the physical space of her campus:

> So the university has what they call "cultural rooms" for each racial and ethnic group on campus. The funny thing is that the African American room is really nicely decorated; it's modern with some contemporary art. The Latino room is the same, with these portraits of these great Latino leaders like César Chávez. The Asian room, when you walk in you see pictures of pandas, geishas, and religious figures [i.e., Buddha]. It's ridiculous! Here we are supposed to have a cultural room and the African American and Latino room are decorated like that and we are exoticized and tokenized.[30]

Notably, even when Indira's university attempted to be racially inclusive in its physical space and decor, it failed miserably because of its complete lack of cultural competence regarding its Asian and Asian American student body. The random collection of what was assumed to be sacred Asian relics further marginalized Asian and Asian American students on that campus. While this is a more overt example than the subtle nuances on most college campuses in the United States, Indira's experience demonstrates the lack of collaborative effort the university put in to create space for Asian American students. White institutional space allows whites to dictate what that campus will look like and how people of color will or will not be included.

Many of our respondents were unable to articulate the campus feel as overtly racialized or overtly hostile. There was "just something about [the university]" that made them feel like outsiders. A large part of it is the physical layout, with that Greek, almost exclusively white, system being at the heart of the campus.

Greek (White) Space

The university is a particularly situated space in which to understand racial processes. Though the university system is presented in discourse as a neutral space, it in fact has a history of racialized practices and a dominant white culture displayed through visible symbols, institutional practices, and organizational spaces. At the university level, where more of a student's time is spent outside of the classroom, the social space and party culture are strong components in the "social transmission of knowledge and power."[31] Specifically, it is through the racialization of spaces that "white power and privilege are reproduced in often tacit and relatively invisible ways."[32] It is through the examination of these spaces that the acceptance of racism on campus can be understood.

Tim, an Asian American junior, describes the pervasiveness of white habitus at the university:

> I can't really say it [the historically white Greek system] hasn't affected me because you go to the quad and you have white fraternities living there and they're the ones who have the parties, they're the ones who host things. So, it's really hard to not be affected by it on some level.

The Greek system at our subject university is heavily white dominated, much like the Greek systems of other colleges.[33] Tim's observation that white Greek life dominates campus life emphasizes the controlling element of white habitus. The racial makeup of the historically white Greek system not only makes it harder for Asian Americans like Tim to gain membership into a white fraternity but also limits the social spaces he can participate in on campus. Tim's admission that it's "hard to not be affected by it on some level" underlines the emotional work students of color must undergo to operate in largely white arenas. The historically white Greek system at this elite Southern university creates a template for white male separation and segregation that marginalizes students of color. The exclusivity of these spaces can reinforce white habitus and color-blind racist ideology among Asian Americans.

This template is not simply restricted to a male fraternity space but is also reflected in white female sorority spaces. Janine describes the racial breakdown of her historically white sorority and other sororities:

> In the sorority I was called back to, there were a lot of Asians. I remember walking past [name of a "top" sorority] room thinking Oh My God they are all blond. It might have been on my part that I felt uncomfortable. . . . They never did anything to make me feel uncomfortable.

Janine interprets feelings of discomfort in the Greek rush process's racial breakdown by putting blame on herself. Julie Park, in a study of Asian American female undergraduates at a predominantly white Southeastern university, found that despite Asian American respondents perceiving sororities to be open to all races, they reported racist instances in the Greek system.[34] Though Janine is a self-identified Asian American activist, she uses a "it's not you, it's me" model minority racial discursive to explain how she felt, which places responsibility for one's successes and failures or unfavorable experiences squarely on the shoulders of the individual instead of on the racial structure. This is a key component of adopting the notions of white habitus. Color-blind racist ideology makes it impossible for people of color to see racism overtly at work. Moreover, Janine's observation is particularly revealing of a larger racialized structure. Though Janine does not say so, the sorority she was called back to where "there were a lot of Asians" was not one of what students at the university refer to as "Core Four," the most desirable social climbing sororities, whereas the "all blond" sorority was a "Core Four" sorority.[35]

Janine's experience is suggestive of a racialized rush process that places white females at the top of the food chain. Similarly, Karen Pyke and Denise Johnson, through interviews with Korean and Vietnamese second-generation women, found that Asian women constructed white women as the successful femininity and produced a dominant-subordinate relationship between white women and Asian women.[36] More simply put, the admittance of "all blond" women to the most desirable sororities and "a lot of Asians" to the lower socially ranked sorority maintains white elite space like the "Core Four" assigned social power to white females over Asians and reinforces white habitus.

Though the white female structure is not equivalent to the dominant white male university culture, it is a system that differentiates power among racial lines to sustain white supremacy.[37]

To maintain this power differential, the few Asian Americans who do gain access to these top historically white sororities may have to sacrifice or hide their Asian American identity. Within the Greek system, a study at a large West Coast university showed that whites were significantly overrepresented.[38] Despite this white dominant reality, a number of respondents at an Elite University also seemed to internalize the white normativity of white sororities. Amy, an adopted Korean American sophomore from the South, refers to Asian Americans joining historically white sororities, saying, "I feel like they're de-raced sort of." Kai, a first-year female Pacific Islander from the West Coast, says about campus sororities:

> I feel that [sororities] are horribly racially segmented. . . . I encouraged my African American friends to rush with me in the normal sorority recruitment like traditional sorority recruitment, I encouraged them, and as much as I thought my roommate actually thought that she would go through all of it, after her first meeting she was like "I'm done with this" because the girls in the sororities just had a different culture so there were a lot more like "peppy happy," you could say, they're preppy as well and so that's not her.

Kai acknowledges sororities' racial segmentation and suggests her African American friends join the "normal" white sorority recruitment in response. In essence Kai suggests that to improve race relations and fix the racial segmentation, women of color should conform more to white realities by joining white sororities. In using the word *normal* to describe white sororities, Kai brands sororities of predominately women of color as aberrant.

Kate, a second-generation Korean American senior, explains how her discomfort with white sororities stems from her "Koreanness": "I never thought about joining a general sorority with whites and diverse, so I think that also branched off of me being more Korean." She refers to the historically white sororities as "a general sorority with whites and diverse." The language our respondents used in their interviews is painfully instructive of how white privilege is associated with a "lack of race." This labeling of majority white sororities and fraternities as "normal" organizations is a color-blind narrative that denies the existence of race to deny racism and also rewrites student-of-color groups as deviant and abnormal.[39] This is symptomatic of the white habitus extending into spaces of people of color. In this case, the color-blind labels proclaiming white sororities/fraternities "nonrace" deny the existence of a racialized space, thus allowing the maintenance of an "invisible" racially segregated white space.

In these white spaces at a predominately white institution, the status of a minority student is a tenuous situation. Amanda Lewis, Mark Chesler, and Tyrone Forman found in conducting interviews with seventy-five African American, Asian American, Latina/o, and Native American students that they felt conflicting pressures to represent their race on campus and assimilate into a larger (white) campus culture.[40] Some studies have suggested that ethnic organizations can be important tools to negotiating a predominantly white social space.[41] Unfortunately, unlike the positive experiences found at other universities, two of our respondents described an Asian American ethnic organization on campus that was itself torn in its identity. Respondents described the Asian Student Association (ASA) as an alcohol-laden social space reminiscent of white fraternity party culture. Janine, an East Coast Chinese American junior, describes her experience with ASA on campus: "I didn't like ASA because I felt that they only focused on Asian things and they were just trying to replicate the frat and whatever thing for Asians and it wasn't really productive." Janine dislikes ASA for its focus on "Asian things" and its imitation of Greek fraternity culture. In an unpublished ethnographic study of Korean student organizations at the University of Minnesota, Stephen Suh describes Asian American organization leaders who felt pressure to cater to non-Asians by offering more cultural programming that superficially highlighted Asian food and dance opportunities.[42] In much the same way, it is possible the university's ASA wins funding opportunities, power, and privilege through this culturally Asian element that is largely consumable and nonthreatening to a larger white university structure. Janine is also put off by the fraternity-like social space created by ASA. Fraternity culture is largely a white-dominated experience. It is possible that these events—and other events that replicate a fraternity culture—would attract Asian American students who would like to participate in a space that imitates white power and privilege, more specifically white masculine power. This imitation or re-creation of white fraternity culture is a product of Asian Americans adopting white habitus, or the ideology associated with it.

Even the possibility of gaining access to favorable racial social spaces elicits constraining negative reactions. When asked about the transition from living in an area with a substantial Asian American population to the Elite University, Jenny, a first-year Taiwanese American from the West Coast, speaks of the university's self-segregation: "Some Asian people only hang out with Asian people.... That's the only thing that I thought was really weird when I came to this campus. Like, why are you self-segregating yourself?" Jenny felt strongly that Asians (her term, which assumedly includes Asian Americans) who were friends only with other Asians was a negative deviant practice. In effect, Jenny uses the term *self-segregation*, often used by "color-blind" whites, to accuse people of color of being exclusionary in nature. She has internalized the language of white habitus and color-blindness and seems not to recognize how having Asian friends and being a part of a racial minority group could be a protective choice against the difficulties of white dominant spaces at the university level.

While some students dealt with exclusion from the white spaces by creating and imitating white space, others felt the need to actually avoid other Asian Americans students. Cindy, a Chinese American senior, states:

> Yes, I definitely like to avoid the Asian people that only hang out with Asian people. I don't want to be classified as being in the same group as them. The majority of my friends are white. And I have my token Asian best friends as well.

The immeasurable power of the hidden curriculum in this white space becomes evident as Cindy wishes to avoid other Asian Americans on campus. There is white power and privilege in this racialized space, and being in an all-Asian/Asian American space is not ideal to Cindy.

Male Space, Sexualized Racism

At the university level, besides a notion of high academic achievement, another dimension of the model minority stereotype is that Asian Americans are "quiet and content with the status quo."[43] In *The Myth of the Model Minority*, Chou and Feagin describe Asian Americans who have internalized this stereotype and deal with racism by ignoring it quietly.[44] Thus, because of the model minority stereotype of quiet Asian Americans, non-Asian Americans could feel free to make overt racist comments to them with little fear of recourse from Asian Americans. Moreover, Asian Americans are often unprepared to deal with the racism in terms that go beyond the individual experience and can find themselves traumatized by overt racism.[45] In such a way, the model minority stereotype and mentality create a positive feedback loop in which non-Asians can make racist remarks without fear of resistance, Asian Americans in a model minority mentality do not actively resist or address racism, and non-Asians continue to make racist comments.

It is important to understand the complicated nature of Asian stereotypes and the referral to them as "good stereotypes." Asian females can exploit racial sexualized stereotypes and racialized sexual desires to gain access to white privilege, but such a privilege can also have associated costs of objectification and eroticized "othering." "Good" Asian American stereotypes have consequences that far exceed their welcome. Furthermore, when faced with overt sexualized racism, a lack of a collective narrative on racism often prevents Asian Americans from even identifying racist situations.[46]

Important to note is that these systems of power are intersecting. While white habitus and color-blind racist ideology support the racial hierarchy, patriarchy and sexism are simultaneously at work as well. For example, when asked about the transition to the elite university from a largely Asian American West Coast community, Jenny first responded that the move had not been difficult. She followed up her answer by relating a story in which she was approached by a group of white and African American males in her dorm common room:

> The football players approached me, "Oh little Asian girl I would definitely love to bang you." And I said, "Oh my god, where am I?"

[Uncomfortable laughing] It was very uncomfortable ... in my dorm ... these boys were not drunk. It was 2pm.... I said, "I'm sorry, I have a boyfriend" and left, but I don't know what, I don't know if they were just trying to ... I don't know what they were doing because they're freshmen [and it was] Orientation Week. I don't know how it is with upperclassmen, but ...

A far cry from an idealized university space, the experience Jenny describes is arguably worse than the racial teasing at the grade school, middle school, and high school levels. Unlike high school, where racial teasing usually concludes by the end of the school day, Jenny experiences this clearly inappropriate comment in a dormitory that is Jenny's residence and home. In a matter of speaking, this male student's comment turns Jenny's home into a hostile racialized space.

Moreover, instead of inserting a form of resistance in response, Jenny incorporates her answer within the context of the model minority. Jenny is almost at a loss for words. She says, "I don't know" four times, and in line with color-blindness she offers two alternative reasons besides racism in trying to explain the racialized experiences. Furthermore, note the word usage the male chooses in his comments. Using the words *little* and *girl* infantilizes Jenny. She is a sexual object to be "banged." The male student's word choice suggests he has consumed or been exposed to media representations and porn imagery/culture of Asian and Asian American females. *Bang* and *little Asian girl* are reminiscent of Asian American female pornography titles like "Bang that Asian Pussy" and "Cute Asian Girl Getting Fucked."[47] In constructing Jenny as a subordinate sexual being, the male student reaffirms his masculinity and sexuality. The situation described ends with Jenny apologizing, "I'm sorry, I have a boyfriend," to the male who made an overtly hostile racist sexual comment. It is quite possible the male will repeat his comments to another Asian woman, being no worse for wear. Sadly, this incident is the second type of overt sexualized racism Jenny experienced. Thus, within the theoretical framework, the football player felt comfortable enough, as much of campus is male space in addition to white space, to approach Jenny without fear of a negative reaction; and Jenny, hampered by model minority mentality, remained quiet and unequipped to deal with this overt racism.

When asked explicitly whether these racialized sexual incidents happen often, Jenny replied, "Not since then, since I do try to keep to myself most of the time with boys because I've had bad experiences with them so far."

With a lack of collective narrative and resistance strategies, Jenny decides to withdraw entirely from this social space. Unfortunately, this avoidance strategy is not effective and is limiting in practice. Jenny cannot avoid all places she is likely to experience sexualized racism, because as examined earlier she is susceptible even in her own dormitory space to objectification and male surveillance.

White Habitus and Racial Preferences in Dating

Dating and hooking-up are widely recognized as important parts of college life. All of the interviewed Asian Americans said they were interested in finding romantic partners in college, but seemed also to recognize certain limitations and boundaries in their love lives. Some of the participants felt that it was specific to the culture of this particular campus. While the women we interviewed generally had an easier time finding potential partners, for both, there was still a certain feeling of racial exclusivity on campus. Diana, a Chinese American senior, explains:

> Yes, I feel like I have much more difficultly finding romantic partners at [the university] than I do anywhere else. I feel like many people at the school are just not open-minded or open to talking to new people. Once they find their cliques, they stick to it and don't venture out to make new friends at all. This applies to romantic situations too. I feel like I've exhausted my pool of potential interests because I haven't met any new people since they're all unwilling to open up and mingle. Maybe I've become more like that too, but the second I leave [the university], I can find so many more romantic interests.

Diana utilizes color-blind language to explain the phenomenon, which we will explore in-depth in the following chapter. It is language like this—that there were clear distinctions, racially, for many of the peer groups—that alludes to the hidden curriculum on campus. When asked about a statistic that Asian Americans are the race least likely to hook up on campus, she replies:

> My gut instinct is to say that the lack of hooking up is because they feel undesirable on campus. [University name] is so self-segregating that Asians here feel like they have to associate with other Asians or they're being white-washed. And yet, if you're not interested in your race's men, then who can you turn to?

Diana asks an important question. With white institutional space, the socialization process of white habitus, and stereotypes coming from the white racial frame, Asian American men are not atop the male hiearchy. She, and other respondents, attributed agency to students on campus because they "self-segregate"; however, absent from the picture is the white racial domination of people of color in this environment. This space on campus has a hidden curriculum that affects all students. In her interview, Diana openly speaks of her preference for white men as potential partners. Asian American women's preference for white men is well documented and part of today's "new racism."[48]

Wade, a Chinese American first-year student, is a perfect example of a respondent who has internalized these implicit messages from the hidden university curriculum. He has gone so far that he has begun to start blaming himself for social pressures and racialized oppression out of his own control:

> Being that you are Asian, it definitely limits you to . . . the amount of different girls you can go for. If you are an Asian guy, girls you can pretty much go for are, like, Asian girls. Going for other ethnicities is definitely much harder. Especially if you don't live in a large metropolitan area, then it's just, like, difficult. It's just not widely accepted, and girls don't consider Asian guys. . . . I think it's just self imposed. . . . I think, like, to some extent my standards are too high.

Wade definitely sees a difference in racialized romance experiences. Through his experiences, he has noted that being Asian means he is "limited" in the different "amount" of girls that he thinks he is able to be romantic with. While he does not explicitly mention what criteria he means by "amount of different girls," he later mentions that Asian men can only be romantic with Asian women, much like how black women were once limited to only dating black men.[49] While he starts out suggesting that his problems are largely a consequence of social and geographic factors (that interracial dating is not as "widely acceptable" for Asian men, and that not growing up in a metropolitan area is a hindrance), he then blames himself for having standards that "are too high."

With this, Wade suggests the internalization of a racial hierarchy that puts whites above Asian Americans. When he was asked if race was a factor in the "obstacles" he faced as part of his romantic life, he responds that the only time race would be an obstacle would be "if the girl were to be white," and that "if a girl was white and I was interested in her that would definitely play an obstacle. A lot of times white girls just aren't interested." Being an Asian and not at the top of the racial hierarchy, he feels that attempting to have a romantic relationship with someone above his racial tier would be too difficult and would present "obstacles." This is extremely problematic, as following seemingly raceless perceptions of beauty and attractiveness has led to internalizing this idea of racial hierarchy.

This racial hierarchy is also articulated indirectly through racial preferences of the Asian female respondents. Like Janice, who found preference for white nerds over Asian males, Alex, a Chinese American third-year student, describes her attraction to "Caucasian guys" over "Asian boys":

> I think I'm just more attracted to Caucasian guys just in general.... Asian men tend to be very androgynous in their features, and I can't date a guy that's prettier than me, and Asian boys tend to be prettier than me.

Notice how Alex phrases her preference for white males over Asian males in terms of masculinity. She refers to Asian males as "prettier" than her and "androgynous" in their features and not handsome. She is able to compliment males as "pretty" and simultaneously deny them masculinity. That is, her adjectives negate the masculinity of Asian males and clearly paint them in feminine terms. This feminizing process does not exist only in the minds of Asian American women; the men in the study also dealt with internalizing these constructions of their masculinity, or what is perceived as a lack thereof. These ideas stem from white habitus, the socialization process of white ideals. These ideals are cemented in the white racial frame, which incorporates emotions, feelings, and images of what is the most ideal type of man or woman. These ideal men and women are racialized, and whiteness is the ideal.

Alex reinforces white hegemonic masculinity not only by relegating Asian and Asian American males to a subordinate position of femininity but also by preferring white males to Asian and Asian American males. Three of the respondents dated only white males, and two of them were in relationships with white males at the time of the interviews. Alex says of Asian female–white male interracial dating, "I feel when Asians and Caucasians date . . . it doesn't feel interracial and I don't really understand why it doesn't but that may be just my personal experience with it."

In this incident Alex has erased the racial line between Asian and white. She is essentially saying that an interracial relationship between Asian females and white males is not racialized and is therefore acceptable in a dominant white hegemonic structure. However, when asked if an Asian male–white female interracial relationship would similarly seem "de-raced," Alex admits, "I think that's actually very different than an Asian female dating a white male. For some reason it has a completely different context and a completely different weight to it." She recognizes the different "weight" or power difference of the Asian male–white female relationship, and though she does not explicitly say it, this pairing is contrary to white male hegemony and thus becomes a deviant interracial relationship. That is, this blurring of the racial lines only works in one way—in favor of the white male. This internalization of hegemonic masculinity and femininity sets a frame of mind where people of color immediately subordinate themselves, become enforcers of other people of color's subordination, and act or believe that they are somehow inferior to whites.[50] This is very clearly seen in the romantic social scene, as Asian American men and people of color in general feel restricted while dating, noting that being attracted to someone of a different race (in particular, whites) may be considered having standards that are "too high." In Chapter 3 we extend this discussion to examine the physical and psychological toll the hidden curriculum of white institutional space has on our respondents.

Conclusion

Asian American participants at this elite university describe a university setting in which Asian Americans can experience hostile racialized white spaces. Asian American organizations imitate white social spaces such as the historically white Greek system to attain honorary white privilege that operates out of the socializing process of white habitus. Color-blind racism is apparent because these mostly white, exclusive organizations are de-raced. Whiteness is invisible and the physical space where the white Greek system is the epicenter rarely gets interrogated. At this university and others like it across the country, Asian Americans are often denied admittance to historically white social spaces like top sororities and fraternities. In 2014 the University of Alabama made headlines for its racist exclusion of African Americans in its sororities. The student body upheld the ruling later in the year to allow the practice to continue.[51] Even in the case of sexualized racism, in which white male preference for Asian women might seem flattering to Asian women, respondents describe how sexualized comments were objectifying and damaging. Overall, Asian Americans in our study were largely ill prepared for resisting sexualized and everyday racism. Asian American females were active agents in perpetuating a white masculine hegemonic structure through racialized dating preferences, and Asian American males internalized the ideology of white habitus by adhering to a racial hierarchy of white racial dating preferences. The Asian American men and women in our sample subtly or overtly internalized the racial tastes, perceptions, and views of the white habitus and used color-blind racist ideology. These tastes shaped by white habitus were not strictly racial. Thoughts and opinion about gender and sexuality were affected by white habitus as well.

Recently an article on college admissions in the Asian American magazine *Hyphen* had a byline that read, "The Hard Part Is Getting In."[52] The hard part may seem like getting in, but the truly hard part is negotiating the white institutional space of the ivory tower as Asian

Americans. Whether they choose to acknowledge it or not, the power of white habitus affects Asian Americans existing in a white-dominated space and takes a psychological toll on the emotional well-being of Asian American students at colleges and universities.[53] Through either resistance or resignation to everyday racism, Asian Americans as individuals exercise much personal agency in either changing or maintaining the white-dominated racial structures that they inhabit.[54]

In today's color-blind era, messages of racial domination become veiled in media, pop culture, and even in micro-interactions within white habitus and extensions of the white spaces outside individual interactions. White habitus, or the "racialized uninterrupted socialization process that conditions and creates whites' racial tastes, perceptions, feelings, and emotions and their views on racial matters," thrives throughout larger institutions, even when those larger institutions are multiracial.[55]

However, there is a need for an intersectional analysis of white habitus and color-blind racism. The experiences of these Asian American respondents that are racialized are intertwined with systems of gender and sexuality. Controlling images that shape perceptions of Asian American masculinity, femininity, and sexuality perpetuates racial domination. Color-blind racism is so powerful because it is hidden in other systems of oppression which are perceived, often, as biologically caused or naturally occurring. These ideas stem from the white habitus, and while whites possess many of these color-blind notions (even if they describe themselves as liberal or progressive), people of color adopt them as well. White habitus is a socialization process for people of color that shapes thoughts and feelings across systems of race, gender, and sexuality. Without the incorporation of these other systems of oppression, our understanding of the white habitus and color-blind racism is incomplete.

We find that even the most educated Asian Americans are not immune to the racist and racialized experiences of the American educational system and social spaces. With this in mind, the university institution must move away from its complacency for Asian Americans and understand that their needs must also be addressed. Robert Teranishi contends that the existing racial structure and systemic racial inequalities in education do, in fact, impact Asian American students.[56] He calls for the need to move beyond an individualism lens and the dominant scripts of hard work and strict parenting that focus on family and culture and tend to ignore institutional practices and inequalities across Asian American and Pacific Islander groups.

The diversity of the population is vast and uncovers the deep structural obstacles that exist for Asian Americans when it comes to higher education, both public and private. Ultimately, the elite university, where more rigorous academic standards are touted as essential, does not protect Asian American students from color-blind racism. Through the systems of gender and sexuality, racist stereotyping and discrimination persist. White habitus shapes whites' perceptions, values, and notions, but it spreads outside of segregated white spaces. People of color are part of the socialization process as well, and whether through interaction with whites, or exclusion, they can internalize color-blind racist ideology.

In Chapter 3 we discuss how Asian Americans use color-blind discourse to describe their racial experiences at university. We also detail how Asian American masculinity and femininity is constructed and how it operates in a racial hierarchy. These accounts illuminate the gendered and sexualized racism faced by Asian Americans. We argue that this gendering and sexualizing process plays a specific role in maintaining the racial status quo. Respondents detail ways in which they were pressured or influenced to meet certain gendered racialized or sexualized expectations. We argue that an intersectional approach to color-blind racism is necessary. White habitus socializes and shapes Asian American students at an elite university through intersecting domains of power and through exclusion in largely white spaces.

Notes

1. Scott Jaschik, "Snow Hate: A Tale of Two Chancellors," *Inside Higher Ed*, January 28, 2014. Retrieved from www.insidehighered.com/news/2014/01/28/u-illinois-decision-keep-classes-going-leads-racist-and-sexist-twitter-attacks.
2. Rosalind S. Chou and Joe R. Feagin, *The Myth of the Model Minority: Asian Americans Facing Racism* (Boulder, CO: Paradigm, 2014); Joe R. Feagin, *The White Racial Frame: Centuries of Racial Framing and Counter-Framing* (New York: Routledge, 2009).
3. Joe Feagin, *Racist America: Roots, Current Realities, and Future Reparations* (New York: Routledge, 2014).
4. Wendy Moore, *Reproducing Racism* (Lanham, MD: Rowman and Littlefield, 2008).
5. Eduardo Bonilla-Silva, Carla Goar, and David G. Embrick, "When Whites Flock

Together: The Social Psychology of White Habitus," *Critical Sociology* 32, nos. 2–3 (2007): 229–253; Eduardo Bonilla-Silva and David G. Embrick, "'Every Place Has a Ghetto...': The Significance of Whites' Social and Residential Segregation," *Journal of Symbolic Interaction* 30, no. 3 (2007): 323–346.
6. Teun van Dijk, "New(s) Racism: A Discourse Analytical Approach," in *Ethnic Minorities and the Media* (2002): 33–49.
7. Moore, *Reproducing Racism*.
8. Feagin, *The White Racial Frame*.
9. Chou and Feagin, *The Myth of the Model Minority*.
10. R.W. Connell and James Messerschmidt, "Hegemonic Masculinity: Rethinking the Concept," *Gender and Society* 19, no. 6 (2005): 845–854.
11. Ibid.
12. Bonilla-Silva and Embrick, "Every Place Has a Ghetto," 340.
13. Chou and Feagin, *The Myth of the Model Minority*; Robert T. Teranishi, *Asians in the Ivory Tower: Dilemmas of Racial Inequality in American Higher Education* (New York: Teachers College Press, 2010).
14. Teranishi, *Asians in the Ivory Tower*, 105.
15. Chou and Feagin, *The Myth of the Model Minority*; Teranishi, *Asians in the Ivory Tower*; Rosalind S. Chou, Kristen Lee, and Simon Ho, "The White Habitus and Hegemonic Masculinity at the Elite Southern University: Asian Americans and the Need for Intersectional Analysis," *Sociation Today* 10, no. 2 (2012); Mia Tuan, *Forever Foreigners or Honorary Whites? The Asian Ethic Experience* (New Brunswick, NJ: Rutgers University Press, 2003).
16. Moore, *Reproducing Racism*.
17. David Eng, *Racial Castration: Managing Masculinity in Asian America (Perverse Modernities)* (Durham, NC: Duke University Press, 2001).
18. Rosalind S. Chou, *Asian American Sexual Politics: The Construction of Race, Gender, and Sexuality* (Lanham, MD: Rowman and Littlefield, 2012).
19. Ronald Takaki, *Strangers from a Different Shore* (Boston: Back Bay, 1998).
20. Chou, *Asian American Sexual Politics*; Yen Le Espiritu, *Asian American Women and Men: Labor, Laws, and Love* (Lanham, MD: Rowman and Littlefield, 2008).
21. Benson Tong, *Unsubmissive Women: Chinese Prostitutes in Nineteenth-Century San Francisco* (Norman: University of Oklahoma Press, 1994).
22. Chou, *Asian American Sexual Politics*; Eng, *Racial Castration*; Espiritu, *Asian American Women and Men*.
23. Sheridan Prasso, *The Asian Mystique: Dragon Ladies, Geisha Girls, and Our Fantasies of the Exotic Orient* (Cambridge, MA: Public Affairs, 2006).
24. Elaine Kim, "'Such Opposite Creatures': Men and Women in Asian American Literature," *Michigan Quarterly Review* 29 (1990): 70.
25. Chou, *Asian American Sexual Politics*.
26. Amy Chua, *Battle Hymn of the Tiger Mother* (New York: Penguin, 2011).
27. Ibid.
28. Eric Margolis, *The Hidden Curriculum in Higher Education* (New York: Routledge, 2001).
29. Chou and Feagin, *Myth of the Model Minority*.
30. Ibid., p. 89.
31. Moore, *Reproducing Racism*, 32.
32. Ibid., 38.
33. Julie Park, "Race and the Greek System in the 21st Century: Centering the Voices," *NASPA Journal* 45, no. 1 (2008): 103–132.
34. Ibid.
35. "Calling All Crazies," *The Truth about Duke*, http://suckmyduke.blogspot.com/ (April 27, 2007).

36. Karen D. Pyke and Denise L. Johnson, "Asian American Women and Racialized Feminities: 'Doing' Gender across Cultural Worlds," *Gender and Society* 17, no. 1 (February 2003).
37. Mimi Schippers, "Recovering the Feminine Other: Femininity, Masculinity, and Gender Hegemony," *Theory and Society* 36 (2007): 85–102.
38. Jim Sidanius, Colette Van Laar, Shanna Levin, and Stacey Sinclair, "Ethnic Enclaves and the Dynamics of Social Identity on the College Campus: The Good, the Bad, and the Ugly," *Journal of Personality and Social Psychology* 87, no. 1 (2004): 96–110.
39. Eduardo Bonilla-Silva, *Racism without Racists: Color-Blind Racism and the Persistence of Racial Inequality in the United States* (Lanham, MD: Rowman and Littlefield, 2006).
40. A. E. Lewis, M. Chesler, and T. A. Forman, "The Impact of 'Colorblind' Ideologies on Students of Color: Intergroup Relations at a Predominantly White University," *Journal of Negro Education* (2000): 74–91.
41. D.A. Guiffrida, "African American Student Organizations as Agents of Social Integration," *Journal of College Student Development* 44 (2003): 304–319; S.R. Harper and S.J. Quaye, "Student Organizations as Venues for Black Identity Expression and Development among African American Male Student Leaders," *Journal of College Student Development* 48 (2007): 127–144.
42. Stephen Suh, "The Korean Student Organization: Institutional Liberalism and the Ethnicity Based Student Group" (2010) [unpublished manuscript].
43. Beverly Daniel Tatum, *"Why Are All the Black Kids Sitting Together in the Cafeteria?" And Other Conversations about Race* (New York: Basic, 1997).
44. Chou and Feagin, *Myth of the Model Minority*.
45. Ibid., 90.
46. Ibid., 151.
47. "Asian Sex Movies," *Redtube*, www.redtube.com (2011); www.huffingtonpost.com/julia-meszaros/elliot-rodger-and-the-effeminization-of-asian-men_b_5401516.html.
48. Chou, *Asian American Sexual Politics*.
49. Patricia Hill Collins, *Black Sexual Politics* (New York: Routledge, 2004).
50. Connell and Messerschmidt, "Hegemonic Masculinity."
51. Mia De Graaf, March 25, 2014, "University of Alabama All-White Sororities Win Right to Remain Racist after Rejecting Two Applicants for Being Black," *Daily News*. Retrieved from: www.dailymail.co.uk/news/article-2588883/Uni-Alabama-white-sororities-win-right-remain-racist-rejecting-two-applicants-black.html.
52. Lin Yang, "The Hard Part Is Getting In: Asian Americans Navigate the Racially Charged Politics of the College Admissions Process," *Hyphen*, 2011, retrieved from www.hyphenmagazine.com/magazine.
53. Chou and Feagin, *Myth of the Model Minority*.
54. Chou and Feagin, *Myth of the Model Minority*, 221.
55. Bonilla-Silva, *Racism without Racists*, 104; Burke, "Discursive Fault Lines."
56. Teranishi, *Asians in the Ivory Tower*.

3
COLOR-BLIND DISCOURSE AND ASIAN AMERICAN SEXUAL POLITICS

In February 2013 over 250 students gathered at Duke University to protest a fraternity party that featured invitations with Kim Jong-il speaking in broken English and party-goers dressed as geishas and sumo wrestlers. With its Asian-costume party, the Kappa Sigma fraternity crossed the line between racial humor and raw insensitivity. Their actions resulted in backlash from the university and gained national media attention. An outpouring of external support from Asian American organizations at other universities and celebrities bolstered the efforts of student activists. And yet, on campus the response was more varied. Within Duke's Asian American community, responses ranged from outraged to apathetic. One student, Johnny Wei, wrote in the student newspaper:

> As an Asian American, I was naturally disappointed in Kappa Sigma's insensitive party theme. I was equally disappointed, however, in how Asian student organizations on campus chose to respond to this crisis.... As Duke's largest minority group, we Asians had the opportunity to take the high road and truly break new ground in eliminating these cultural insensitivities, a problem that seems to plague Duke perennially.[1]

The Kappa Sigma party is a prime example of the racialized social landscape that undergraduates traverse, and the mixed reactions that followed demonstrate the complexity of racial ideology. Asian Americans champion education as a pathway to success that transcends race.[2] The university is viewed as a way to earn one's way to the top and escape a system of racial bias. Yet, even as Asian Americans become a greater proportion of the university population, little effort has been given to understanding their university experiences. In the rare instance when they are included in racial discourse on higher education "they have been reduced to a single, stubborn persistent narrative—as a 'model minority.'"[3] A few notable articles describe Asian American experiences with physical violence and verbal harassment in high school and college.[4] Fewer studies still have examined the social context and romantic relationships of Asian Americans at university.

In this chapter we place Asian American undergraduates in the driver's seat, exploring the language they employ to cope with, survive, and negotiate their social experience at a predominately white institution. The discourse Asian Americans use to make meaning of their racialized and sexualized relationships reveals the complicated positionality of Asian Americans as a "racial middle." On one hand, they are seen as "forever foreigners," but on the other hand, being stereotyped as a "model minority" or "honorary white" may encourage Asian Americans to use color-blind racist discourse to explain their positions on campus and legitimize racist hierarchy.[5] Stereotyping as either "forever foreign" or "model minorities" sets Asian Americans apart from white college students. To understand the meaning behind these practices, we interrogate the intersectionality of race, gender, and sexuality and the particular racialization of this group. We contend that elite campus culture, as white institutionalized space, leads Asian Americans socialized in this environment to adopt these racialized messages, thus creating sometimes tense Asian American sexual politics between straight-identified Asian American men and women. We also detail how Asian American masculinity and femininity are constructed and how these definitions operate in a racial hierarchy. Our respondents describe ways in which they were pressured or influenced to meet certain gendered racialized or sexualized expectations. These accounts illuminate the gendered and sexualized racism faced by Asian Americans. We argue that this gendering and sexualizing process plays a specific role in maintaining the racial status quo.

The Role of Discourse in Color-blind Racism

As explored in Chapter 1, color-blind racism allows the racial status quo and more specifically whiteness to go uninterrogated. Color-blind racism principally operates through the expression of conversations, media, and other forms of communication. There are numerous parts to communicating color-blind racism, but we highlight three of its discursive practices: (1) the use of certain semantics to express racial views, (2) the almost complete incoherence when it comes to certain issues of race, and (3) the minimization of concerns about racial inequality.[6]

To adapt to the shift from Jim Crow racism to post–Civil Rights era realities where openly racist statements were no longer socially acceptable, color-blind discourse opted for specific language to express racial views. For example, one might couch a racist statement by emphasizing that it is not a racist comment. One might also use descriptors that are tacitly racialized such as describing a neighborhood as "ghetto" when they mean to say it is a minority community. The incoherence regarding certain issues of race is sometimes characterized by long pauses, and "I don't know" statements. Such incoherence obfuscates intelligent rational conversation on racial themes. It also makes difficult the ability to recognize and resolve racist experiences. Color-blind discourse minimizes concerns about racial inequality not only by denying racial structure via incoherent discourse but also silencing those who raise the issue. As an example, individuals might call Asian Americans outraged by racial discrimination "too sensitive" or "overreacting," in essence minimizing racism as an emotional problem. Embedded in the subtleties of talk, color-blind discourse may appear benign compared to the system of fear and violence that Jim Crow racism employed. However, color-blind discourse could be more powerful for its tacit hegemony, moving through the minds of the majority and minority alike.[7]

Subordinated minorities are not immune to adopting and internalizing parts of color-blind racism. Claire Jean Kim is one of the seminal critical race scholars to offer a structural framework to expand beyond "black and white" and consider the racial position of Asian Americans.[8] She criticizes racial hierarchy for its one-dimensionality, which assigns status and privilege to whites at the top, blacks at the bottom, and other minorities like Asian Americans in the middle. Kim instead maps out white racial hierarchy on two axes: an axis of racial superiority/inferiority, and an axis of insider/foreigner. In a position of "near whiteness" Asian Americans might be more likely to identify and promote white interests than other people of color. Effectively the racial triangulation of Asian Americans drives a wedge between themselves and other minorities. However, we maintain that the two axes are not enough. When analyzed through an intersectional lens, systems of gender, sexuality, and class complicate the simplified racial order that Kim outlines. Bonilla-Silva theorized a "tri-racial" model that includes class as a marker in determining racial superiority and inferiority, but he fails to address the racial shuffling that occurs when including stereotypes of gender and sexuality.[9] Kim and Bonilla-Silva offer a critical analysis. Our work extends Kim's map of racial hierarchy and Bonilla-Silva's tri-racial modeling toward a more intersectional approach, suggesting gender/sexuality as an additional axis to understand Asian American racial discourse.

Asian American Sexual Politics

Current Asian American racial formation and identity theories are inadequate. Racial analysis of Asian Americans is incomplete without consideration of gender and sexuality constructions. Connell and Messerschmidt coined the term *hegemonic masculinity* to describe the ideology of male dominance.[10] White hegemonic masculinity constructs the white heterosexual male as the version of normalized manhood, whereas men of color are cast into weaker "subordinated masculinities." Compared against a standard of whiteness, men of color have their masculinity constructed as pathological. Subordinated masculinities are racially specific. For example, Asian American men receive a particular placement on a gendered racial hierarchy. They must negotiate normalized white constructions of masculinity differently than their Latino or African American male counterparts.[11] Racial stereotypes can and do change over time, but they continue to maintain the racial status quo.

As we noted earlier, the stereotyping of early male Chinese immigrants was similar to past and current constructions of African American men as hypersexual, aggressive, and dangerous.[12] The Asian American male stereotype gradually changed. Now Asian American men are often portrayed as hyposexual, impotent, and weak.[13] Hegemonic femininity works in a similar fashion, promoting white women over women of color, though both are still subordinate to white men. White hegemonic ideology shapes not only our understanding of masculinity and femininity, but also our romantic and sexual preferences.

We contend that Asian American sexuality is formed in ways that perpetuate white privilege, particularly for white men. Controlling images of both Asian American men and women exist "to define the white man's virility and the white man's superiority."[14] Again, at the core of these Asian portrayals is the strength of white hegemonic masculinity. Defining white male virility and superiority through demeaning representations of Asian Americans is essential in retaining the existing racial structure. Further, the principal distributor of these stereotypes is discourse. More specifically, public discourse such as media, politics, and education are the most powerful modes to transmit these depictions. It is no accident that these forms of public discourse are predominately controlled by white elites.

Racialized Love

Higher education is a particular space where Asian Americans undergo racial identity management while exploring their romantic preferences.[15] Dating and romantic relationships are widely recognized as important parts of college life.[16] Asian American out-dating has been increasing rapidly while Asian American out-marriage is declining.[17] The racially exploratory nature of dating, especially in regard to Asian Americans, has been suggested as the reason behind this trend. This makes dating in an elite university, itself an exploratory space, an excellent setting to investigate the role of race in romantic interactions.

Patricia Hill Collins defines sexual politics as "a set of ideas and social practices shaped by gender, race, and sexuality that frame all men and women's treatment of one another, as well as how individual men and women are perceived and treated by others."[18] Moreover, it is in the manner in which these social experiences and ideas are talked about that offers an intimate analysis of how love and relationships are built. What we argue is that Asian Americans' social experiences and ideas at HWCUs are shaped by white habitus, the white racial frame, and white institutional space. The relationships between Asian Americans and their non-Asian American peers are shaped by the campus climate, which is part of the larger racialized society. Asian Americans often view the elite college campuses, these HWCUs, as enlightened places where they can form friendships and relationships free of racial bias. Our data suggests that race is still a salient factor in the social experiences of Asian American students at university.

Our research interrogates the intersectionality of race, gender, and sexuality, and the unique position of Asian Americans at HWCUs. Though our data alludes to a problematic white university culture in which whites engage in sexualized racism with little consequence (as we outlined in Chapter 2), we find equally worrisome the emotional management Asian Americans must perform to deal with such racism. We document how Asian Americans utilize language to negotiate the realities of sexualized racism and racialized romantic preferences. We find that our respondents pull from the white racial frame when they discuss their racial preferences in partners. The hidden university curriculum includes learning that the most ideal romantic or sexual partners are whites.

At university, a persistent stereotype of Asian Americans is that they are "quiet and content with the status quo."[19] In the *Myth of the Model Minority*, Chou and Feagin describe individuals who have internalized this stereotype and deal with racism by ignoring it quietly. Our research documents Asian American undergraduates resorting to a color-blind discourse that prevents them from articulating the racialized nature of certain social experiences.[20] The discursive strategy also at times leaves them unprepared to deal with and process racism. This ultimately creates a harmful positive feedback loop in which non-Asian Americans make racist remarks, Asian Americans in a color-blind discursive do not actively resist or address racism, and non-Asian Americans continue to make racist comments without fear of backlash.

Asian American Females as the Eroticized Other

As discussed in the previous chapters, racist comments that rely on so-called good stereotypes such as the "model minority" should not be prematurely dismissed as complimentary; their nature is far more complicated. Oftentimes, when faced with overt sexualized racism, a lack of a collective narrative on racism prevents Asian Americans from even identifying racist situations.[21] For example, when asked about the transition to an elite university from a largely Asian American West Coast community, Jenny, the first-year Taiwanese American female we met in Chapter 2, responded that the move had not been difficult, but then followed up her answer by relating a story in which she was approached by a group of white and black males in her dorm common room who made overtly racist and sexist comments to her.

When asked explicitly whether these racialized sexual incidents happen often, Jenny replied that she has made a conscious decision to avoid spaces like the club scenes due to her negative racialized sexual experiences. However, she and other survey respondents described the emotional work they have to perform in order to deal with these comments. Lindsay, a Chinese American female first-year student, considers

> people who say things like I'm a "sexy Asian" or something. I guess I am shallowly complimented, and then I get annoyed because there shouldn't be this discrepancy between "sexy" and "sexy Asian."

Lindsay raises the point that the "compliment" to her says something more specific about her race. For example, she is sexy *because* she is Asian or *in spite of* it. In this example, what may seem like "positive stereotyping" of an Asian American woman is another demarcation of racial difference. Susan, a Chinese American female senior respondent, explains the psychological toll of sexualized raced comments: "It made me feel violated and that they are only looking at me from a sexual and very primitive point of view." Susan keys into the way the male gaze has the power to control; using the adjective "violated" to describe how she feels in response to the male gaze, Susan suggests a trauma or form of emotional violence. We argue that this sexualized and gendered trauma is racialized in the white institutional space of the elite university. Numerous universities across the country have recently made headlines because of their "rape tolerant" cultures.[22] This culture is a result of white institutional space being protective of white men, and we suggest that analysis of this campus culture includes race.

The males who make these racialized sexualized comments restore their hegemonic masculinity by objectifying the Asian American female in a racialized way. They also play on a history of racial imagery of Asian females as hypersexual exotic creatures to be rescued or entangled with white males. Embedded in a color-blind world of racism without racists, non-Asian male commentors might see these raced sexualized comments as "compliments." However, these examples of sexualized racism work purposefully to establish the hegemonic masculinity of the commentators, subordinate Asian American females, and leave an emotional toll.

Exoticised Other in Romance and Relationships

Sexualized racism becomes more complicated in the context of relationships and romantic love. Our data documents the ambivalence and emotional guesswork that our respondents negotiate in their interracial relationships, particularly in regard to "yellow fever." This is a phenomenon in which white men prefer Asian or Asian American women because of preconceived notions about their exoticized sexuality, subservience, and submissiveness.[23] The stereotyping of Asian and Asian American women is firmly rooted in the white racial frame.[24] The constant negotiation of preconceived notions of Asian American exoticized sexuality in romantic relationships was particularly problematic in the respondents' partner selection. Survey respondent Mary says:

> I feel fairly conflicted about the relationship between my race and my sexuality. At [Elite University], "yellow fever" is fairly prevalent, and many people openly admit to this. The stereotypes applied to Asian women in particular are not necessarily positive—e.g., freaky girls who want to rebel against their traditional parents or girls who want to let loose after being repressed for so long. Although I'm fine with both my sexuality and my Asian identity, I'm always sensitive to the possible stereotypes

that others might be applying to me. For example, if I get hit on at a bar and the person makes reference to my racial identity, I tend to be put on guard.

Mary highlights the frequency of "yellow fever" and the acceptability for "people to openly admit" to it. Yet, she also speaks about a weariness of being targeted as an Asian female stereotype and tendency to "be put on guard." At first glance, the prevalence of this exoticized Asian female stereotype seems to advantage Asian American females.

When asked whether being called "exotic" bothers her, Kai, a Pacific Islander American female sophomore, said, "No, I like it. I eat it up." Throughout her interview, Kai asserts her pride for her Pacific Islander heritage. Her positive reaction to being called exotic could stem from her pride in her racial identity. However, Kai goes on to make clear how being exoticized by her romantic partner led her to end the relationship:

> The fact that I was [a Pacific Islander] came up all the time.... This one guy I was seeing . . . this is kind of why I left him; I swear to God he just loved me because I was the [Pacific Islander] chick and he could just tote me around as his. I tend to take it in stride. I'm like okay, yeah, maybe I am [Pacific Islander]. If that makes me oh so much more desirable to you great for you, but you would have to know me more than that. I don't know.... Like, you know when guys go on vacation and they get to hook up with that exotic girl and they talk about it all the time? I'm pretty sure he did that. I'm not positive, but I have a pretty good idea that he did.

Kai ended her relationship with her partner because he treated her as an exoticized Pacific Islander and not as Kai, the person. Herein lies the problematic nature of "yellow fever": the high sexual desirability placed on Asian American and Pacific Islander women may appear a positive social position, but it also can give way to sexual objectification and racialized sexual desire. It facilitates relationships in which the Asian American females are viewed as sexual caricatures rather than people. Even threat of "yellow fever" creates a shadow in interracial relationships. Janine, a Chinese American junior, says in regard to her white boyfriend,

> I feel very like those "Asian women are sexually something or whatever." I feel it makes me feel insecure about how people perceive me especially in relationships, whether those thoughts ever enter my boyfriend's mind. So I don't want to be treated like an object and I don't want to be a victim of "yellow fever" or anything like that.

Janine speaks to the romantic questioning that she negotiates in response to "yellow fever"; she is on her guard that she may be racially sought out even with her boyfriend, in her intimate partnership. Chou writes, "There is no real test to accurately determine the motives that are not influenced by societal constructions."[25] The exposure to "yellow fever" leaves Asian American females continuously wondering.

Asian American Male Double Consciousness

Continuous media and public discourse depicting Asian Americans in subordinate stereotypical roles may also contribute to the internalization and even the belief in harmful stigmas associated with being Asian American. While images of Asian American women in the media objectify them as exotic sexual beings, Asian American men are "racially castrated."[26] As an Asian American individual who has internalized hegemonic masculinity begins to reflect negative feelings toward his minority group, he oppresses himself through feelings of negative self-worth. This is extremely harmful, because it can lead to problems with double consciousness—a recognition of Asian American characteristics as abnormal or inferior, while also recognizing one's own Asian American identity.[27] After being exposed to racialized mocking and stereotypical images of Asian American men on television, Daniel—a gay second-generation Taiwanese American senior, recounts his uncertainty and dislike for his race:

> I tended to think that Asian guys are not really that attractive to other people—to other guys. And, I think that Asian guys in media, too, are portrayed as more effeminate, unless you look at martial arts or whatnot—in a lot of cases, not in all cases. . . . So I struggled with that a lot, and I would say that I still struggle with that in terms of my own attractiveness to other people. And I think there's always been some kind of

jokes, or stereotypes about Asian guys and cock size, things like that. But, I did struggle with that a little, because I did look kind of like the stereotype that was placed on us, and one that I thought would possibly be true, and not having a comparison, besides porn, where everyone had huge cocks, you know, you're not really sure.

Daniel's experiences are not uncommon compared with other responses given by Asian American men interviewed. *All* of the men interviewed mentioned that they were unsatisfied with the way Asian American men were portrayed in the media, and *all* mentioned that they had to negotiate the stereotype that Asian men have small genitalia. Though they tended to play down the impact of this stereotype, the fact that every single participant mentioned it makes it worthwhile to investigate, especially as sexualized insults are central to the making of contemporary adolescent masculinity.[28] Previous research found the same widespread dissatisfaction with the media and sexual stereotypes of Asian American men extending well beyond college.[29] Men in the study were ages eighteen to seventy, and had all experienced some form of harassment from other men and, sometimes, women challenging their masculinity.[30]

If there are widespread preconceptions that Asian American men have small penises, and no easy way to refute these stereotypes, these respondents may have to continually confront this problematic phallocentric masculinity. Being surrounded by these disparaging depictions of Asian American masculinity in the media can cause serious issues of self-worth. Daniel mentions that he "struggled a lot" with the portrayals of Asian American men as "not attractive" and "effeminate," and that he still deals with those internalizations to this day. Daniel's negative internalizations of his race eventually put him through an identity crisis in which he starting hating his own race:

> I really had trouble [with] or disliked being Asian at one point, and thought there was a lot of pressure associated with it and didn't really care for it. . . . I didn't think of my friends as people, I didn't necessarily know anyway, because I just didn't have that much experience, and it was just kind of difficult in that sense to navigate socially what I was looking for in my friends.

This concept of racial self-hate, or rejection of Asian Americans by Asian Americans, is very apparent in Daniel's words. He makes clear that his feelings of negative self-worth were tied to his "dislike of being Asian." This can have far-reaching effects into other parts of life. For example, Daniel had a hard time navigating the social scene at his school and really questioned what he was looking for in his friends. Ted, a Chinese American sophomore male, also spoke about how media messages inform our understanding of masculinity and beauty. When asked, "Do you feel Asian American bodies are attractive?" Ted responds:

> Compared to the mainstream culture here, no. I don't really know how to describe it, but if you compare a typical Asian American face, and what's considered to be a more attractive American face, the features are definitely sharper in the American. The bone structure is different. A lot of Asians, well this is really bad, but they have a nerdy look to them. You know what I mean.

It can be assumed that Ted means white when he compares an "American" face to the "Asian American" face. Images of white hegemonic masculinity deny the attractiveness and desirability of Asian American males on basis of race. These ideologies come from a white racist frame that is an integral part of white institutional spaces like elite universities. Moreover, it is such a powerful ideology that Asian American males internalize and must negotiate this feeling that Asian males are less attractive and "nerdy." Asian Americans are continually faced with the crisis of understanding and being aware of the negative implications of one's race while simultaneously identifying with their race. This double consciousness is a constant emotional burden on Asian Americans from day to day and cumulatively adds up to a large psychological toll.[31]

Racial Romantic Tastes and the Adoption of the White Racial Frame

All of the interviewed Asian Americans said they were interested in finding romantic partners in college but also seemed to recognize certain racial limitations and boundaries in their love lives.

Our Asian American female respondents' racial preferences insinuate the influence of racial hierarchy in romance. Diana, a Chinese American female senior, explains:

I look for predominantly white males as partners, specifically those who are over 5'10" in height, with similar education level, and [who] are career ambitious. I prefer white men because they are more independent and don't have a tendency to be as needy as Asian men in relationships. Also, my mom has somewhat encouraged me to seek white men because she believes they are more likely to take on equal child-rearing responsibilities. My mom has always complained about how my father did very little to raise me and my brothers. But, in general, I prefer white men because they're more aggressive in all aspects of life, more independent, and are more readily seen as successful. I also feel more attractive when I'm dating someone white, though it's hard to explain why. I guess in a way I'm more proud to show off my white boyfriend than my Asian boyfriend. I just feel slightly more judged when I'm dating someone Asian, and feel more prized when I'm dating someone white.

Diana uses two frames to reason her preference for white males as romantic partners. The first frame of reasoning relies on seeming cultural differences; she describes her mother's warning about the archetypal chauvinistic Asian male, unwilling to take responsibility for domestic and family responsibilities. The second frame stems from hegemonic masculinity. White men are "more aggressive" and "more independent"—essentially more masculine—whereas Asian males are "needy" and subordinated.

Moreover, Diana says white males "are more readily seen as successful." Diana is perhaps alluding to the "bamboo ceiling" that impedes Asian males from moving up the corporate ladder because they are stereotyped as weak, quiet, and unable to lead. She acknowledges that white maleness comes with economic privilege. The economic racial mobility she mentions has been translated into romantic preferences. Diana admits she "feels more attractive dating someone white." Though she says "it's hard to explain why," she goes on to say she "feels more prized when I'm dating someone white." In essence, she benefits from white privilege and power in having a white partner. By association with whites she as an Asian female becomes "more attractive" and "more prized." In preferring white males, she participates in the subordination of Asian American males while she herself moves up the racial hierarchy by dating white males.

While it is tempting to shrug off racial romantic preferences as natural or accidental, they are in fact guided by a larger racial hierarchy and are political in nature. When asked how her white family would react to her dating an African American male, Amy, an adopted Korean American sophomore, says the following:

> I feel like growing up in the South my mom's never been big on black or Hispanic people. Asian, white, whatever is okay. I think she'd be okay with anything but I guess she says, like, "I don't see how they'd be attractive." Sometimes she's like, "I'm not attracted to them so I don't know whether you would be or not."

Though Amy describes her partner preference based on the person, not the race, her white mother negatively describes African American and Hispanic males as unattractive and implies that they are less desirable. In so doing, the mother discourages her daughter from dating African American and Hispanic males.

It is not simply white families who perpetuate a racial romantic structure. When Alex, a female Taiwanese American sophomore, is asked what would happen if she brought home an African American male as her potential partner, she states, "I don't think my family would be like 'oh no you can't do that,' but it would definitely be a source of discomfort." This source of discomfort she describes is not simply due to the fact that she would be dating interracially but directly because her partner would be African American. Previous research has documented the prevalence of Asian Americans and their parents adopting racist stereotypes of blacks and Latinos.[32] The white racial frame is pervasive, and "model minority" stereotyping creates cleavages between these groups of color; thus, many parents of Asian Americans may discourage their children from these kinds of interracial relationships.[33] People of color occupy different positions within the racial hierarchy in a gendered and specific way. The tension and discomfort that Alex describes between Asian and African American dating is a result of a racial hierarchy favoring whites. This becomes even more apparent in the case of "yellow fever."

Yellow Fever

As we noted earlier in this chapter, "yellow fever" is a phenomenon in which white men prefer Asian women because of preconceived notions about their exoticized sexuality, subservience, and submissiveness. In 2009 the women's magazine *Marie Claire* published an article on white wealthy male–Asian female relationships. The article described Asian females as "exotic arm candy" and emphasized the fetishized nature of these racialized relationships.[34] The constant negotiation of "yellow fever" and preconceived notions of Asian exoticized sexuality in romantic relationships was particularly problematic in our respondents' partner selection.

At first glance, the prevalence of this exoticized Asian female stereotype seems to advantage Janine. She describes how easy it is for her to "hook up" with white male partners and her experience with "yellow fever": "I made out with a guy [who] maybe now I realize had yellow fever because all his girlfriends, everybody he pursued [was Asian] and I guess it was oddly easy to hook up with him." In this case, Janine did not know at the time that this "hook up" partner had "yellow fever" and only has unconfirmed suspicions after the fact. For her, the preferences that some white males have for Asian women facilitates her interactions with white males. In the short-term hook up, Janine mentions suspicions of "yellow fever" in benign terms. In her long-term relationship Janine's reaction is quite different:

> I was really mad my first boyfriend was yellow feverish. . . . I always suspected . . . it would fit the stereotype to be yellow fever and the girlfriend after me was Chinese, yeah, but then that could have just been a function of my high school was 50 percent Asian and him being a nerd because there is this weird hierarchy that puts Asian women with white nerds.

In this incident Janine expresses anger that her boyfriend had "yellow fever." She is mindful to contribute an alternative reason for his partner selection—the large Asian female student body—but she also emphasizes the power differential between Asian American women and white "nerds" in relationships that privilege white males. It should be noted that these white "nerds" are often privileged over Asian males, because some Asian American women (like Janine) only date white males. Even without the existence of intent, the hegemonic white masculine structure and its representations of the Asian female as submissive and sexually exotic must be negotiated and questioned in approaching interracial relationships and questioning the motivations of loved ones.

In terms of racialized experiences, several respondents mentioned their encounters at night clubs. Amy talks about being warned about the party scene by another Asian American female undergraduate. "I started going out to [name of club] . . . and they were like . . . since you're Asian you're going to have to be on the lookout. . . . All races are going to come after you because you're an Asian girl." Essentially, Amy's friend cautioned her to be on her guard from everyone while at a club because she may be racially sought out. Such high sexual desirability placed on Asian American women may appear a positive social position, but it also can give way to sexual objectification and racialized sexual desire.

Racial Castration and Psychological Costs for Asian American Men

While Asian American women are stereotyped as exotic, sexualized racial others, Asian American men are stereotyped as asexual, effeminate, foreign, weak marginalized men.[35] Color-blind racism can be hidden within the confines of other systems of oppression. With controlling images of Asian bodies, male and female, prevalent in the discourse, there can be a psychological toll. In Rosalind Chou's *Asian American Sexual Politics*, one respondent, Irwin, illustrates how external messages about his gendered race affected his self-image; he had a difficult time identifying with masculine constructions:

> I've either emasculated myself or given myself a different identity as an adult male. I've thought of myself as something other than what you think of when you think of the word "man," "guy," a "male," a "dude," whatever, but not a man. Obviously I think it has something to do with my environment. When I say that, I mean that I took what was around me and believed it. I internalized all of that.[36]

Irwin's environment was very much a white habitus. The definition of *manhood* is based on white hegemonic masculinity; this was also the case for the Asian American men in our sample on this university campus. The intersection of race and gender for Asian American men, like Irwin, can be so stigmatizing that they may internalize the stereotypes about themselves. The effects of color-blind racism can psychologically damage people living in this society.[37]

Irwin describes being able to be both negatively and positively influenced by representations of Asian Americans. Whites benefit from consistent positive portrayals in the media. They consistently see images of white heroes and saviors in movies.[38] There are numerous examples of whites in diverse types of roles, but people of color see these images much less often—and that is a key component to white habitus and the white racial frame. In essence, the largely white-owned media is another source of the white racial frame and color-blind racist ideology. The men in our research have grown up in a world where media is racially segregated and exclusive. The images they see of Asian American men are limited to roles where they are "geeks" or "nerds" and rarely the handsome, strong hero. At university, these Asian American men must interact on campus with peers who have also repeatedly seen these narrow media portrayals of the Asian American male.

Conclusion

Asian Americans may be ready to engage in the academic rigors of university, but our data suggests they are less prepared to navigate the white institutional social space of the ivory tower and the white racial framing that is entrenched in HWCUs. Whether they choose to acknowledge it or not, the double consciousness of being Asian American and existing in a white-dominated space takes a psychological toll on the emotional well-being of Asian American students at colleges and universities. We analyzed narratives that demonstrate how the intersection of racial and gender identity affects the self-image and self-esteem of these Asian American students. The women, while seemingly more desirable to men on campus, must confront racialized gender stereotypes that exotify them. Even in cases of sexualized racism in which white male preference for Asian women might seem to advantage Asian women, respondents described how sexualized comments were objectifying and traumatic. The male respondents have few positive examples of Asian American men in the media, and must address issues of self-image and self-confidence while dating in this white space. Asian Americans as individuals perform emotional work in either challenging or maintaining the white-dominated university spaces.

Asian American undergraduates in our study describe a university setting in which Asian Americans experience hostile racialized spaces. In examining the speech Asian Americans use to describe these social settings, it is evident that their color-blind discourse perpetuates overt and/or covert everyday racism. Color-bind discourse leaves Asian Americans ill-equipped to address racism. Moreover, it invites more racist comments into the fold because a racist commentator can feel confident that Asian Americans targets will not retaliate. Overall, Asian Americans on campus faced the emotional challenges of resisting and resigning to sexualized and everyday racism.

We argue that the elite college campus is a white institutionalized space where Asian American females are confronted with a white masculine hegemonic structure through racialized dating preferences and Asian American males internalize the racial hierarchy of racial preferences at psychological cost. We have found that even the most educated Asian Americans are not immune to the pervasive racism and sexism found in the American educational system and its social spaces. We demonstrated the intersectional nature of racism, particularly how it is sexualized and gendered. With this in mind, universities must move away from their complacency regarding Asian Americans and understand that the culture is in want of reconstruction, beginning with its social spaces and student interactions.

In Chapter 4, our data reveal how sexual and romantic relationships are formed, and we examine the dynamics of Asian American intraracial and interracial relationships. We provide a review of relevant theories important for understanding how Asian American students at an elite university navigate a multiracial romantic landscape. Particularly, we highlight what the extant literature has to say about the role of racial structure and different types of capital in informing the decisions of Asian American social behavior. We also examine these ideas empirically and present findings concerning Asian and Asian American students' attitudes about interracial romantic relationships. Respondents balance messages from their families and external racialized forces. From these forces, a hierarchy of partners based on race, ethnicity, class, and gender emerges. Respondents discuss relationship hardship and success. We further expand on Asian American male "racial double consciousness." Most notably, both male and female respondents speak positively about their bodies when they seem *less* Asian American and closer to "white" features.

Notes

1. Johnny Wei, "An Asian-American's Response to the Backlash against Kappa Sigma," *Duke Chronicle*, February 6, 2013. Retrieved from www.dukechronicle.com/articles/2013/02/07/asian-americans-response-backlash-against-kappa-sigma.
2. Rosalind S. Chou and Joe R. Feagin, *The Myth of the Model Minority: Asian Americans Facing Racism* (Boulder, CO: Paradigm, 2014).
3. Robert T. Teranishi, *Asians in the Ivory Tower: Dilemmas of Racial Inequality in American Higher Education* (New York: Teachers College Press, 2010), 11.
4. S. R. Rosenbloom and N. Way, "Experiences of Discrimination among African American, Asian American, and Latino Adolescents in an Urban High School," *Youth and Society* 35, no. 4 (2004).
5. Mia Tuan, *Forever Foreigners or Honorary Whites? The Asian Ethic Experience* (New Brunswick, NJ: Rutgers University Press, 2003).
6. Eduardo Bonilla-Silva, "The Linguistics of Color Blind Racism: How to Talk Nasty about Blacks without Sounding 'Racist'" *Critical Sociology* 28, no. 1 (2002): 41–64.
7. Teun van Dijk, "New(s) Racism: A Discourse Analytical Approach," in Simon Cottle (ed.), *Ethnic Minorities and the Media*, 33–49 (Milton Keynes, UK: Open University Press, 2000).
8. Claire Jean Kim, "The Racial Triangulation of Asian Americans," *Politics and Society* 27 (March 1999): 105–138.
9. Eduardo Bonilla-Silva, "From Bi-racial to Tri-racial: Towards a New System of Racial Stratification in the USA," *Ethnic and Racial Studies* 27, no. 6 (2004): 931–950.
10. R.W. Connell and James Messerschmidt, "Hegemonic Masculinity: Rethinking the Concept," *Gender and Society* 19, no. 6 (2005): 845–854.
11. Chou, *Asian American Sexual Politics*; David Eng, *Racial Castration: Managing Masculinity in Asian America (Perverse Modernities)* (Durham, NC: Duke University Press, 2001).
12. Ronald Takaki, *Strangers from a Different Shore* (Boston: Back Bay, 1998).
13. Yen Le Espiritu, *Asian American Women and Men: Labor, Laws, and Love* (Lanham, MD: Rowman and Littlefield, 2008).
14. Elaine Kim, "'Such Opposite Creatures': Men and Women in Asian American Literature," *Michigan Quarterly Review* 29, no. 70 (1990): 69.
15. Rosalind S. Chou, *Asian American Sexual Politics: The Construction of Race, Gender, and Sexuality* (Lanham, MD: Rowman and Littlefield, 2012).
16. Elizabeth A. Armstrong, "Sexual Assault on Campus: A Multi-Level Integrative Approach to Party Rape," *Social Problems* 53 (2006): 483–499.
17. S. Sassler and K. Joyner, "Social Exchange and the Progression of Sexual Relationships in Emerging Adulthood," *Social Forces* 90, no. 1 (2011): 223–245.

18. Patricia Hill Collins, *Black Sexual Politics* (New York, Routledge: 2004), 6.
19. Beverly Daniel Tatum, *"Why Are All the Black Kids Sitting Together in the Cafeteria?" And other Conversations about Race* (New York: Basic, 1997), 161.
20. Chou and Feagin, *The Myth of the Model Minority*.
21. Ibid.
22. Caroline Heldman and Danielle Dirks, "Blowing the Whistle on Campus Rape," *Ms. Magazine* 24, no. 1 (2014).
23. B. Kim, "Asian Female and Caucasian Male Couples: Exploring the Attraction," *Pastoral Psychology* 60 (2011).
24. Chou, *Asian American Sexual Politics*.
25. Ibid., 94.
26. Chou, *Asian American Sexual Politics*; Eng, *Racial Castration*.
27. William Edward Du Bois, *The Souls of Black Folks* (Chicago: A.C. McClurg, 1903), 186–187.
28. C.J. Pascoe, *Dude, You're a Fag: Masculinity and Sexuality in High School* (Los Angeles: University of California Press, 2007), 25–39.
29. Chou, *Asian American Sexual Politics*.
30. Ibid.
31. Wendy Moore, *Reproducing Racism* (Lanham, MD: Rowman and Littlefield, 2008).
32. Chou and Feagin, *The Myth of the Model Minority*.
33. Ibid.; Chou, *Asian American Sexual Politics*.
34. Ying Chu, "The New Trophy Wives: Asian Women," *Marie Claire*, 2009, retrieved from www.marieclaire.com/sex-love/advice/asian-trophy-wife.
35. Chou, *Asian American Sexual Politics*.
36. Ibid., 107.
37. See William H. Grier and Price M. Cobbs, *Black Rage* (New York: Bantam, 1968); Abraham Kardiner and Lionel Ovesey, *The Mark of Oppression: Explorations in the Personality of the American Negro* (Cleveland: World Publishing Company, 1962); Verna Keith et al.; Joe R. Feagin and Karyn D. McKinney, *The Many Costs of Racism* (Lanham, MD: Rowman and Littlefield, 2003).
38. Hernan Vera and Andrew M. Gordon, *Screen Saviors: Hollywood Fictions of Whiteness* (Lanham, MD: Rowman and Littlefield, 2003).

4
INTRARACIAL AND INTERRACIAL RELATIONSHIPS

Introduction

On the night of May 23, 2014, Elliot Rodger went on a killing spree, targeting sorority women at nearby University of California, Santa Barbara. While many news outlets focused on Rodger's mental health issues, a few reports mentioned the intersection of class, race, gender, and sexuality.[1] Rodger was a self-proclaimed "un-kissed virgin," was sexually frustrated, and felt that the half-Asian part of him was responsible for it. His first three victims were all Asian American men (two were his roommates, and one a visiting friend of theirs); Rodger killed them while they were sleeping. He left his apartment in hopes to exact a "war on women," where he would "punish all females for the crime of depriving me of sex."[2] After Rodger's spree was over, six people were killed and thirteen wounded. Rodger left behind a manifesto that highlighted his feelings of rejection and inadequacy, largely because he had little success with women, which he blamed on being part Asian American.[3]

As we hope we have demonstrated thus far, systemic racism is a foundational piece of US society. People of color, throughout various stages of their lives, endure racial stereotyping rooted in the white racial frame and other forms of racial discrimination. When constantly being taught a hidden curriculum, throughout all stages of education, Asian Americans—like whites and other people of color—can and will adopt racist ideology. Whites believe it to be normalized ideology, and they can fail to interrogate white privilege and power. People of color may resist or internalize the messages. When people of color internalize racist messaging it can thus impact self-image and self-esteem. This internalization, we argue, may affect Asian American sexual politics. Our respondents, while sometimes critically analyzing their racial preferences in dating, often just see their relationship choices as color-blind preferences. In this research and in previous monographs, Asian American men have voiced frustration with their media portrayal, dating options, and the ease with which Asian American women attract partners of various races.[4] Elliot Rodger demonstrated similar frustrations, and while his actions convey that he is an extreme case, systemic racism and the white racial frame have an effect, whether real or perceived, on intraracial and interracial relationships.

In this chapter, our data reveal how sexual and romantic relationships are formed, and we examine the dynamics of Asian American intraracial and interracial relationships. Respondents balance messages from their families and external racialized forces. There is a hierarchy of partners based on race, ethnicity, class, and gender. Respondents discuss relationship hardship and success. The male respondents share experiences that highlight how "racial castration" occurs in the socialization of Asian American men. Asian American women are met with an exotification and Orientalization as sexual bodies but are also awarded a unique empowerment that is not as available to their male counterparts. We summarize our findings and discuss their implications, drawing larger conclusions about how race and gender operate in the lives of Asian Americans.

Intraracial and Interracial Relationships

Interracial relationships, especially marriages, have nearly always been viewed as a bellwether of race relations in the United States.[5] Milton Gordon argued, in his pioneering and widely cited book, *Assimilation in American Life*, that intermarriage marked the final stage of assimilation to American culture and that rises in intermarriage were evidence of diminishing social distance, prejudice, and discrimination between racial groups.[6] However, much of the discourse on interracial marriage is based on research involving black/white couples, with little attention devoted to the navigation of racial dynamics "inside" and "surrounding" these relationships. This situation has resulted in lack of understanding of two areas: the role of race and its corollary "isms" in how individuals come to choose partners, and the position of other racial groups besides blacks and whites in navigating these relationships.

With the increasing racial and ethnic diversity in the US population, it is not clear that our limited understanding of racial dynamics within black/white couples applies to romantic interracial pairings involving Latinos, Asians, or other groups. Insights about the role of race within interracial Asian and white couples are particularly noteworthy. Asian Americans have been considered a "model minority" for nearly seventy years, during which some Asian American social indicators have risen to a point where they parallel whites.[7] For example, Asian American median income now surpasses that of whites.[8]

The rate of interracial marriage for Asian Americans increased from the 1960s to the 1980s, though it has declined over the past several decades.[9] This trend is not consistent with other racial groups, whose rates of interracial marriage have continued to increase.[10] Given this anomaly, it seems imperative to explore current attitudes about race in interracial pairings among Asians and whites. We are particularly interested in investigating the attitudes and language that Asian and Asian American college students use to approach and navigate these relationships in ways that move beyond specifying whether those attitudes are a reflection of diminishing prejudices between the groups.

By focusing on dating as a form of exploratory romantic relationship, research can investigate the ongoing navigation of romance before larger decisions such as marriage are made. In an interracial context, dating is extremely important to consider, as dating patterns do not always mirror marriage patterns. For example, Asian American out-dating has been increasing rapidly while Asian American out-marriage is declining.[11] The racially exploratory nature of dating, especially in regard to Asian

Americans, has been suggested as the reason behind this trend. Dating often occurs during university schooling, and elite university student bodies are purposefully constructed to "promote diversity" through minority representation. Thus, the timing and social environment offer a somewhat unique space for interracial interaction, including interracial romance. Additionally, the elite university is a space where Asian Americans undergo racial identity management while looking for romantic partners.[12] This makes dating in an elite university an excellent space to investigate the role of race during romantic interaction, especially interracial romance.

In this chapter we examine Asian American undergraduate students' approaches to and understanding of interracial romance, particularly with whites. We consider these issues in the context of four conceptual perspectives: social exchange theory; hegemonic masculinity and femininity; racial double consciousness; and race and gender intersectionality. We show how Asian and Asian American students make conscious decisions to uphold elite university white habitus, the importance of racialized family expectations, and the existence of a dating/marriage framing contradiction. These findings are important because they investigate an emerging paradigm in race relations and may inform future race relations in the day of a more multiracial and ethnically diverse America.

Social Convergence among Asian Americans and Whites

As we consider how Asian Americans navigate their romantic lives in a multiracial space, especially with whites, it is important to understand the relative social position of the actors involved. Understanding Asian American social positioning relative to their most common interracial romantic partners, whites, is a piece of the sociopolitical landscape of relationships. While Asian Americans make up only 5 percent of the nation's population, they are growing in numbers as well as socioeconomic status. Several demographic indicators suggest that Asian Americans are doing very well in America: They have a higher median income than any other racial group,[13] and they have the highest rates of achieving a college degree compared to other racial groups.[14] Following the Immigration Act of 1965, the United States has seen a huge increase in the number of foreign-born Asian Americans, and the median income of Asian Americans has surpassed that of white non-Hispanic Americans in the last several decades. It is from such achievements that Asian Americans have often been labeled the "model-minority."[15]

As Asian status indicators rise, it seems Asian American political interests have been aligning with traditionally white interests as well. In some public discourses, Asian Americans are now considered a "non-disadvantaged" minority.[16] They are excluded from many types of racially based scholarships and admissions programs just as whites are. This has caused much public opinion to suggest that Asian Americans are "hurt" by affirmative action, as are whites. Residentially, Asian Americans also show less segregation with whites than with blacks.[17] In a recent study of Asian American intergroup relations, Asians as a group responded that they were more comfortable "getting along" with whites than any other ethnic group, including their own.[18]

Asian Interracial Romance: 1960s to the Present

Asian and white romance has mostly been studied in the context of interracial marriages. Since the 1960s, when the Supreme Court ruled antimiscegenation laws unconstitutional, studies have revealed several major trends in Asian American intermarriage. First, Asian American intermarriage rates climbed steadily from the 1960s into the 1980s. However, since the 1990s there has been a notable drop in Asian interracial marriage.[19] This drop coincides with a large increase in Asian American immigration brought about by the Immigration Act of 1990. Yet Asian American interracial marriage rates are still the highest of any US racial group. In a study of newlyweds in 2008, nearly one-third of Asian Americans surveyed married someone of a different race/ethnicity.[20] Those who out-marry are mostly likely to intermarry with whites. In 2008, newlywed Asian Americans had whites for their partners at a rate of 75 percent. Moreover, Asian American out-marriage varies by group. Japanese and Filipinos have traditionally out-married the most while Indian Americans have out-married the least.[21] Harry Kitano suggests this is due to the unique history of many Asian ethnicities in the United States.[22]

An additional point of consideration is that Asian American women tend to out-marry at a higher rate than Asian American men. This is the opposite of patterns that exist for black and Latino populations, where the men out-marry at higher rates.[23] In 2010 Asian women–white man couples outnumbered Asian man–white women couples by a factor of three.[24]

Four Relevant Theoretical Perspectives

Social Exchange Theory

Most theoretical explanations of interracial relationships draw upon the idea of social exchange. Romantic relationships can be represented as exchanges of capital, generally social or economic.[25] Particularly in the case of ethnic minority men and white women, the theory suggests the men give up economic capital while the women give up social status (race caste). In the case of white men and minority women, the theory suggests the men give up social caste, while the women give up sex.[26] These relationships tend to progress faster into sexual activity perhaps due to this exchange. Minority-white pairings also lead to cohabitation faster, perhaps due to societal rejection of interracial relationships.[27]

Central to social exchange theory is the concept of multiple types of capital for exchange. As Pierre Bourdieu suggested, different types of capital exist based on social configurations. Besides social, economic, and symbolic capital, other types of capital exist within the scope of relationships, particularly interracial relationships.[28] The presence of such capital can be observed through what individuals suggest are ideal attitudes or features to have through their dating behaviors. For example, there exists a clear notion of phenotypic capital, where among people of color, phenotypic features associated with white hegemonic beauty are idealized. For example, many Asian Americans mention their eye shape (too small) and their skin tone (too dark) as features they are not proud of.[29] There is much evidence of language capital as well, where language and speaking accents are also hierarchized. For example, American English with an upper-class accent is considered superior to accented English, which is respectively superior to other languages, particularly those native to countries from the "Global South." Another apparent form of capital is in framing, where a "white racial frame" affirming the white centric status quo is dominant over other nonwhite ethnocentric frames, or a progressive "social activist" frame.[30]

The multiplicity of capital and the negotiation of its use are crucial to the understanding of interracial relationships. In the case of interracial relationships between a white person and a person of color, it is already understood that the person of color commands valued capital to negotiate exchange for the white's race caste capital.[31] Recognizing additional forms of capital relating to interracial relationships helps inform choices that individuals make when approaching interracial relationships.

However, social exchange theory does not consider agency—that is, while individuals may indeed gain or lose capital based on the formation and maintenance of a relationship, this exchange is not necessarily explicitly stated or negotiated.[32] It does, however, depend on the existence of a disparity in capital—a hierarchy, in which certain individuals gain advantages for certain traits that may be inherited (e.g., skin color) or learned (framing). The current study will not look at relationships, but attraction. Thus, while individuals may be motivated knowingly or unknowingly by the ideas of social exchange, no exchange itself will be analyzed.

Hegemonic Masculinity and Femininity

Navigating gender structure generally involves the theory of hegemonic sexualities, the idea that certain masculinities and femininities exist that provide cultural and social capital, and that are culturally and socially superior to other subordinated masculinities and femininities.[33] These masculinities and femininities are resoundingly white, upper-class, and straight, while subordinate sexualities are poor, colored, and nonheterosexual. This theory of a hierarchy of physical sexualities complements Eduardo Bonilla-Silva's tri-racial model, in which he suggests the formation of a three-tiered hierarchy where US inhabitants gain social capital as a result of their skin color.[34] Whites gain the most benefit, followed by lighter-skinned minorities like some Asians and some Latinos, while blacks and darker skinned racial minorities suffer the most.

The hierarchy of hegemonic sexualities complements the idea of multiple romantic capitals. While phenotypic capital is most obviously implied in the structure of hegemonic sexuality, other types of capital have their place in hegemonic sexuality. For example, language capital carries weight in attraction—different accents and languages have respective disparate values. For example, while European accents, particularly British accents, have been romanticized, Asian accents have been discounted. Additionally, ideological framing carries romantic weight: traditional gender role frames have been appreciated while more progressive framing has been depreciated. This is clear even in Connell's writing about "emphasized" femininity as opposed to "hegemonic" femininity. In this framework, to gain the most structural advantage, women must always recognize their position subordinate to men. In relation to racial minorities, this is also the case as racial minorities who do not question or defend the racial status quo generally receive more privilege than those that do not.

Individuals with more phenotypic capital are awarded certain privileges and mobility in society, especially in places that institutionally promote white centricity. While the historically white elite university is a multiracial and ethnically diverse space, it has been shown to reproduce white supremacy.[35] Previous studies affirm that Asian Americans are subject to this white institutional pressure and are adversely affected by it, though many Asian students integrate and perpetuate this system.[36] For example, Chou and colleagues in previous analysis of the data we use for the current study found that while some resist white centrality and others resign to it, all self-identifying Asian students required some level of emotional management to function in a space that subordinates Asian sexuality and racial identity.[37]

Racial Double Consciousness

Discussions of minority racial identity generally touch on the idea of racial double consciousness (RDC), which W. E. B. Du Bois coined in the early twentieth century.[38] RDC purports that blacks struggle with two contradictory concepts—one recognizing their blackness, and another equating blackness with inferiority. The cognitive dissonance that ensues is a source of negative mental health, which can manifest as myriad health and identity problems. Though double consciousness is commonly confined to discussions on race, it is a concept that applies to all subordinated and oppressed identities: the poor, the nonstraight, and women, as well as all people of color.

Racial double consciousness exists through the maintenance of a white habitus—the lifestyle, values, and dispositions that shape everyday interaction between individuals. As Bonilla-Silva describes it, white habitus is a "racialized, uninterrupted socialization process that conditions and creates whites' racial taste, perceptions, feelings, and emotions and their views on racial matters." The presence of white habitus is ubiquitous at the elite university.[39] People of color in elite universities must manage and navigate white habitus on a daily basis—conforming and resisting on both conscious and unconscious levels. In our prior research, we found that all of the Asian and Asian American students we interviewed spent emotional energy either resisting or resigning to the implications of white habitus.[40] For those who identify as Asians and Asian Americans, the presence of counter-narratives rejecting Asian inferiority is common as well.

In a previous study, we discussed the elements of racial double consciousness apparent to Asian Americans in an elite university setting. It was clear that all Asian student respondents understood both elements of white habitus and an ethnocentric counter-narrative—however, the usage of each differed from respondent to respondent.[41] In this study we further examine how this duality (holding both white habitus and ethnocentric narratives) affects the decisions of Asian students, especially in decisions involving race in romance.

Intersectionality and Interracial Relationships

In *Black Sexual Politics*, Patricia Hill Collins suggests that race and gender have overlapping and combinatory effects, such that different combinations of gender and race are constructed differently.[42] The perspective is termed *intersectionality*. In her examples of controlling imagery, Collins shows how sexuality for black men and sexuality for black women are constructed differently. She uses this to explain the different histories of how black men and women have been treated in the United States. It is also used to explain disparity in social behavior, such as how black men out-marry at a higher rate than do black women.[43]

Intersectionality has been used to explain the different patterns that exist in Asian American male and female sexuality.[44] Historically, Asian men and women have been socially constructed with different controlling images.[45] As we noted earlier, the first Asian immigrants—largely manual laborers—to the United States were stereotyped as aggressive and hypersexual, especially toward white women. As immigration grew and men looked to other forms of labor for jobs, they became constructed as castrated and weak-willed. Later, Asian American women arrived in large numbers; they became exotified as either dangerous "dragon ladies" or delicate "china dolls." Although these images seem different, the creation of each emphasized the white man's virility.[46]

Drawing on these historical images, we argue here that intersectionality explains disparate attitudes and approaches toward interracial romance among Asian American men and women. For example, the pattern of reverse out-marriage (where Asian men out-marry less than women) can be explained through the almost universal "castration" of Asian American men since the 1960s, whereas Asian women have been subjected to more sexualized constructions.[47] This is counter to more current constructions of other men of color (particularly black men and Latino men), who have been relatively oversexualized.[48]

Intersectionality entails different positions for people of color on a hegemonic sexuality hierarchy. This means that across races, people of color gain different levels of capital based on their gender, and vice versa. Collins recognizes how this contributes to black gender disparity in different economic sectors: for example, black men are largely eschewed from the service sector due to being constructed as overly masculine and dangerous.[49] In other words, black men lack a "comfort" capital that black women have relatively more of. In *Asian American Sexual Politics*, Chou suggests that Asians, and particularly Asian women, have been awarded certain social capital based on their race/gender characteristics.[50]

People of color are placed in different locations on a hegemonic sexuality scale. This structure is similar to Bonilla-Silva's tri-racial model of America. Racial minorities closer to whites, who gain honorary white status and privilege, are more likely to navigate the white racial frame and white supremacist ideologies. In prior research, we have found that Asian Americans, particularly East Asians in elite universities, use color-blind ideology and white racial framing in their narratives, as well as show high levels of racial double consciousness. We suggest that having honorary white privileges (especially those afforded by hegemonic sexualities) correlate with white racial framing and result in racial double consciousness. We suggest that Asian American students with greater levels of racial double consciousness, especially in relation to concepts of hegemonic masculinity/femininity, are more likely to be involved in interracial romance with whites.

Based on the four theoretical perspectives, we contend that the respondents in our sample behave in ways that reflect their honorary white position in Bonilla-Silva's tri-racial model. As a racial group that receives some benefits of "white privilege," they work to maintain the white centricity of hegemonic sexuality. This is bolstered by the composition of this sample as mostly educationally elite East Asians. While they experience some dissatisfaction through racial double consciousness from their "othered" status, they do not challenge the maintenance of white habitus while dating in the elite Southern university. Data analysis revealed three themes of importance relative to understanding Asian American students' attitudes and experiences around race and interracial dating: (1) racialized family expectations, (2) the manipulation of capital, and (3) the Asian dating and marriage frameworks.

Racialized Family Expectations

Asian Americans are extremely cognizant of how their romantic partners align with their often racialized family expectations, and they tend to use the concept of Asian parenting and upbringing in understanding their racial identity. These expectations generally fall along similar guidelines, including dating within one's ethnicity, a skin hierarchy based on whiteness, and an economic prosperity. These expectations form an "Asian parenting/upbringing" frame of Asian identity—it is consistently in their minds when they navigate romance. Nearly all respondents were cognizant of their parents' expectations toward their own romantic partners (only two did not report any mention of preferences). When talking about what considerations they had for potential romantic partners, many respondents mention their familial expectations. Students also often used this frame of "Asian upbringing" to interpret racial disparity as it relates to Asians—for example, using it to explain why Asian American dating/hook-up prevalence at college was low relative to other racial groups.

The respondents recognize their parents' wishes for their romantic partners to be not only of the same racial group but also the same ethnicity. These parental preferences would be classified as a "counter-frame" to the dominant white racial frame; specifically the "home culture" frame.[51] As Asia's peoples are vast and diverse, this probably reflects a wish to preserve cultures and norms understood by a specific group of a certain region.[52] Shruti, a study participant who is Indian American and a senior at the university, says this: "My family has an understanding that they would prefer that I marry someone of the same caste and from the same region of India as me. There are no specific occasions that illustrate this idea because it is just so understood." Shruti's parents specify that their preferred partner for Shruti would be of Indian descent and also of the same caste—a further identity qualification beyond ethnicity.

Every respondent who mentions the reason behind these expectations says they had to do with a cultural understanding. Eric, a Chinese American senior, explains: "My parents would prefer that I marry a Chinese girl, since from their perspective, it simplifies the culture gap." Others' mention of parental expectations suggests that marriage outside one's ethnicity would "create problems." If their children could not find a partner of the same ethnicity, sometimes the same racial group would do. Tim, a Chinese American sophomore, reveals: "Yes, my entire family seems to prefer that I date a Chinese girl, or at least another Asian." The foremost preference that Asian and Asian American parents show for their own race and ethnicity largely informs the ethnocentric "Asian upbringing" frame that places value on Asian identity. This shields partnerships from anti-Asian framing such as the white racial frame, and the resulting racial double consciousness that could result. However, this is not without nuance, as there seems to be a hierarchy of preference within the Asian racial group as well. Other researchers have also found that Asian Americans have been pressured by their parents to adhere to an Asian hierarchy for dating, for example,

Chinese over Japanese.[53] This hierarchy is largely due to past military contention between these home countries in Asia.

At the intersection of ethnocentricity and white centrality, the "Asian upbringing" frame involves hierarchies of Asian ethnicities, based on skin tone and historical domination. In particular, it seems that East Asians discriminate against their South Asian sisters and brothers. Jaimee, a Chinese American senior, shares: "Well, one parent doesn't want me to date people who are 'darker' than me—so Indian, Latino, and black." This focus on skin capital in Asian families finds its way into the current generation's ethnic preferences as well. Lucy, a Taiwanese American senior, reports that her parents and friends thought she should stick with "an Asian boy." Her partner, identified as Indian, might qualify as Asian in certain contexts but not in all. Particularly when it comes to romance and marriage, Asian Americans recognize the many lines of ethnicity that divide them. The clearest divide between East Asians and South Asians is defined phenotypically, through skin tone.

Danny, a Southeast Asian American sophomore, explains that his East Asian American girlfriend held some of the same views about his ethnicity: "The fourth [partner] (Korean) was very nice to me, but I always felt like she thought of my nationality (Vietnamese) of being lesser than hers. She would sometimes joke about cultural/national insignificance of my ancestry. Asian on Asian discrimination, man." The Asian upbringing frame is often used to validate skin and ethnic hierarchy through history and "ancestry." As the Asians and Asian Americans in this study consisted completely of first- and second-generation immigrants, their parents' nationalist and ethnocentric values are often tied with Asia-centric hierarchies that pit Asian ethnicities against each other. These intraracial politics are a part of what it means to be Asian and Asian American, and are constantly navigated in the form of the Asian upbringing frame.

The Asian upbringing frame's intraracial skin hierarchy is compounded by an even stronger distaste for dark-skinned minorities, especially blacks and Latinos. Tom, a "Yellow" (self-identified) senior, says that "My dad literally sat me down one day out of the blue and was like, whatever you do, just don't bring home an Arab girl." Asian American parents often do not even consider other non-Asian people of color to be possible romantic partners for their children. Amanda, a first-generation Korean American first-year student, explains this of her familial expectations:

> I get the feeling that they would not like to see me with an African American or Hispanic boyfriend although they have not told me so specifically. Whenever I tell them about a male friend, they always want to know if he's white or Asian. They never ask if he is African American or Hispanic.

Amanda's parents did not even consider that someone she would be interested in dating might be black or Hispanic—when inquiring about possible partners, "he" can only be "white or Asian." While some may argue this preference for whites above other non-Asian racial groups can be explained by the Asian cultural preference for lighter skin, it is more possible this represents an alignment with the more globalized white-centric hegemonic sexuality. Historically, preferences for whites as romantic partners increased drastically in conjunction with western domination and colonization of Asian countries.[54] To this day, whites in Asian countries benefit from privileges afforded to them by a century of rape, economic and political domination, and psychological colonization by their white ancestors.[55] In the Asian upbringing frame, much consideration is given to the skin capital of whites, which can compensate for the Asian cultural capital that whites lack.

Economic and educational capital is also a prominent consideration in the Asian upbringing frame. Tina, a Taiwanese American junior, comments: "[My mother] has often said aloud that I (and my sister) should marry a doctor or a lawyer, and expressed concerns about my sister's engagement to someone (who is Caucasian) who lacks financial security." This consideration for professionals, especially the educated elite, is probably a reflection of the specific Asian/Asian American population reflected in this mostly East Asian sample. These elite university students have parents that are referred to as the "brain drain," the best and brightest of their respective countries who generally accumulated much economic or educational capital themselves before immigrating to the United States.[56] In some cases, this emphasis on economic stability trumps all. Kelly, a Chinese American junior, notes: "[My parents] have no preference on race or ethnicity, but they expect a high education level and career path." Darker-skinned Asians or minorities are generally only considered if they have generous amounts of other capital, particularly economic and educational. Alice, a Chinese American senior, says this: "My mom always said that anyone is fine as long as he is not black, unless it's a super successful black guy who has a sense of family and responsibilities. And of course no Japanese people, but that does not even need to be stated." Here we see interaction between various considerations of the Asian upbringing frame, in which economic stability can "compensate for" a lack of ethnic cultural capital. However, there seems to be no method to ameliorate the intraracial ethnic divide—here, a historical Chinese-Japanese antipathy.

Respondents used this "Asian upbringing" frame to understand their family expectations. Some respondents reported no explicit mention of preferences but still assumed the same racialized expectations of their romantic partners: of the same ethnicity, and the opposite gender. Lucy, a Taiwanese American senior, indicates this about her family's expectations: "Though my parents never said it right out, I always knew that they would prefer for me to be with a Chinese/Taiwanese guy. Regarding career, they obviously want me to either be a doctor, lawyer, or CEO (pretty typical of Asian parents)." There is no doubt in Lucy's mind (she "always knew") that her parents conformed to the stereotypical Asian family expectations, regardless of whether they explicitly mentioned it. Perhaps Lucy had assumed her parents' romantic expectations to be in line with their career expectations, which she calls "typical of Asian parents." Lucy's understanding of romantic racial politics helped her make sense of why her parents and friends were disapproving of her romantic relationship.

Additionally, participants used the Asian upbringing frame to explain Asian racial disparities. For example, Asian Americans in elite universities are often associated with academic rigor at the expense of romantic or social engagement. Several students explicitly explained this phenomenon as a result of the Asian upbringing. Johnny, a Chinese American junior, notes:

I believe that many Asian Americans have been influenced by their upbringing to prioritize study and work above all else, so they devote less time to other endeavors. Because of this, however, some may have not have developed the social skills needed to hook up or initiate relationships.

Johnny recognizes the Asian upbringing as a source of socialization—it is because Asian Americans "have been influenced by their upbringing" that they show certain patterns in dating. This specific realization is counter to other participants, who attributed certain behavior patterns of Asians to inherent tendencies. Alice comments:

A lot of [Asians] are super shy and do not put themselves out there. Asians also tend to be super studious. Those two factors combined are not very conducive to finding hook ups or relationships. If they fix those two things—have more confidence in themselves and go out more—then it should not be a problem.

The difference in these explanations is in the source of the problem. While Alice is quick to characterize her race as "super shy" and "super studious," she does not mention why. Later, she suggests these characteristics are things that are "problematic," and could be "fixed," implying inherent deficits. Johnny, in comparison, recognizes the influence of an environmental and social condition. In this case, Johnny's views are representative of the Asian upbringing frame while Alice's are more typical of a white racial frame. Parents are perhaps the most influential family members to an individual in terms of racial framing. For Asian Americans, their familial expectations inform how they navigate dating and romance, or even explain their racial identity in the form of an Asian upbringing frame.

Manipulation of Capital

Our results indicate that Asian Americans manipulate their available capital when looking for potential romantic partners. Most of our respondents participated in methods that align with hegemonic sexualities confirming white centrality. Asian American students recognize the benefits of being publicly seen with whites, and they make an effort to whiten their social spheres, thereby increasing their social capital. Additionally, our findings showed that respondents internalize anti-Asian perspectives of beauty that are white-centric and hegemonically affirming. This is most obvious when students talk about their own physical features, often reconciling their unfavored features as "Asian." The data analysis also revealed that some students uphold a frame of Asian accomplishment, whereby Asians in America had "made it" past the point of being a disadvantaged minority. We argue that these behaviors are white habitus enforcing, and in cases where social exchange occurs, a manipulation of held capital that results in gaining white privilege, regardless of intent.

Capital Gains through White Social Settings: Avoiding other Asians

Elite universities have been described to be highly social settings. In addition to academics, college life is largely defined by partying, romance, and other social activities.[57] In this setting, students' social interactions are strongly shaped by their available capital—what resources can they leverage—which includes social capital (e.g., who one is networked with). In elite universities such as the one described in this study, white institutions are abundant and powerful.[58] Networks that include whites are thus empowered, and people of color can gain social capital when networked with whites. Respondents tended to "play up" their white-including networks when entering social settings. Cliff, a Vietnamese American first-year student, notes: "If I could choose, I would like to hang out with more white people. There's a pressure in the sense that if you can hang out with white people, then you fit in." Cliff's desire to be networked with more whites emphasizes the hierarchy that exists within an elite university. His wording suggests that networking with whites requires ability that some Asians do not possess: "if you can" network with whites, you will "fit in."

Most of the respondents enforced this hierarchy, though only some explicitly recognized it. Shruti highlights the connection between the historically white Greek life institution and certain Indian students who are privileged by white networks:

> There is a pressure to avoid being associated with the Indian group of students on campus. Indian people who hang out with

Caucasians are respected more than those who hang out with Indian people. I think this is because they are more connected with the Greek life hierarchy than the rest of the Indian people.

Shruti finds that Indians who network with whites are respected more across racial lines, perhaps due to the pervasiveness of the white racial frame in elite universities. What is more, she raises the important consideration of the elite university's historically white Greek institution. As researchers of the elite university suggest, historically white Greek institutions hold a position of social power on elite university undergraduate campuses, as they play a large role in the hegemonic partying environment of an elite university.[59] Additionally, they sometimes receive desirable campus space and location, and sanctions from administrative penalization.

Moreover, study participants recognized the stigma of having "too many" Asian friends. Sherry, a Chinese American senior, tries to avoid being classified as an Asian who has Asian friends: "Yes, I definitely like to avoid the Asian people that only hangout with Asian people. I don't want to be classified as being in the same group as them. The majority of my friends are white. And I have my token Asian best friends as well." In Sherry's framework, there are two distinctions of Asian American students: "tokens," who maintain a primarily white network; and self-segregators, who maintain a primarily Asian network. Crystal, a Korean American senior, mentions that she occasionally feels uncomfortable in locations with other Asians: "I kind of feel uncomfortable being part of a large group of Asians—it's that self-segregating stereotype." Asian Americans, like other people of color, are often more conscious of their social surroundings because they transition more frequently between spaces that are white-dominated versus minority-dominated. However, due to the pervasiveness of the white racial frame, some Asian Americans see white-dominated groups as "normal" versus the "uncomfortableness" of an Asian-dominated group. Eric says: "I tend to not hang out with too many Asians at once, although that is because it gets personally overwhelming for me, rather than out of fear of any social stigma." Though Eric implies he is not afraid of any "social stigma," he is still "overwhelmed" in Asian-dominated spaces, suggesting he internalized an "anti-Asian" white racial frame regardless of reason.

Pressure to Flock Together

A small number of respondents also mentioned the presence of another frame where there was social pressure against too much white contact. Tim notes: "There is usually a pressure to hang out with Asian Americans and at the same time to not hang out with these groups. Depending on whom you hang out with, you're pressured in either situation." His comments suggest the presence of a counter-frame against the white racial frame, where Asians affirm themselves as normal and recognize their lowered social status in a white-centric setting. Though they may not be recognized as such, these social groups in college act as support networks for people of color dealing with racial double consciousness.[60] Jaimee says she can "identify with" her Asian friends more: "I mainly hang out with Asians—I do tend to clump towards them because I can identify with them more, and I'm happy that way." It is likely that Jaimee's Asian friends connect with her more due to not only cultural similarity but also a similar lowered social position in a white habitus space.[61]

Duality of Pressure

However, the pressure to associate with whites is not monolithic among Asian Americans. Several respondents also noted a more ethnocentric pressure to associate with one's own race as well. Jimmy, an Asian American first-year student, says:

> There are derogatory terms such as "white-washed" and "fobby" (or "foppy") to describe Asian Americans sometimes. The former refers to one who has given up most or all of his/her cultural background and has limited/only trivial knowledge of his/her ethnic/cultural roots. The latter indicates someone who hangs onto his/her cultural ties very strongly and can be very "socially awkward" when trying to learn/adopt other cultural norms.

This duality of pressures is very evident for Asian Americans who have friend groups that are both Asian-dominated and white-dominated.

Due to the social fluidity that certain Asian Americans have, they are subject to hierarchical pressure from both a pro-Asian and a pro-white perspective. Ester, a Chinese American senior, indicates:

> At [school], I feel pressure either way I turn. Now that my friends are mostly Asian, I feel pressure to avoid spending time with so many Asians. But once I spend too much time with others outside of my race, I feel pressure from the Asian community to reassociate with my race. It's like I can't win either way.

This duality of pressures can result in a hopelessness for those who choose to "straddle" both groups: "It's like I can't win either way." As a form of racial double consciousness, it is a scenario unique to people of color who must navigate white-dominant spaces, but it is especially relevant for those with the social capital to access white spaces, such as elite university East Asians.

Internalizing White Hegemonic Standards of Beauty

Another manner in which Asian Americans maintain the white habitus of elite universities is through the internalization of white-centric hegemonic sexuality. While most Asian American undergraduates responded that they were satisfied with their bodies, a majority of respondents used language that showed signs of internalizing white hegemonic standards of beauty. In these cases, the satisfaction with one's body features was often given in relation to a measurement standard for Asians, resulting in a formulaic statement relative to a "racial standard," that is, "I am satisfied with my body because I am ____ for an Asian." Eric, a self-identified Chinese senior, followed this formula, leading with an affirmation of satisfaction, yet following this statement with a comparison to the "Asian" body:

> I'm very satisfied with my body. I'm particularly tall for an Asian, so I think that has a lot to do with it. I'm athletic, but not overly muscular, and I guess part of me wishes I could gain more muscle mass, but that's more of a cosmetic concern than anything else, and it does not trouble me too much. My biggest dissatisfaction would probably be my eyes, which are fairly small and slanted. I've learned to be okay with it, but I do wish they were bigger.

When Eric mentions his favorite feature, he claims that that it is his height "for an Asian," not just simply being tall, that has "a lot to do with" his satisfaction for his body. His dissatisfaction with his body is also based on an understanding of beauty that frames Asian-ness as an undesirable standard: his "not overly muscular" body and "small and slanted" eyes are cases of undesirable stereotypical Asian characteristics.

In many cases like this, Asian Americans have internalized a distaste for certain characteristics that they have been taught are undesirable by the white racial frame. As a result, they tend to find pleasure in not falling into such stereotypes that define people of their color. A Chinese senior commented about her body: "Yes, I am satisfied with my body. Asians are perceived to be small/tiny, super skinny, and have small eyes. I think I'm pretty different and don't really fit into that stereotype." Though this student claims she is satisfied with her body, she immediately follows it with the fact that she doesn't fall prey to stereotypes that other Asian American women presumably do. While not explicitly stated, it may not be too presumptuous to conclude that her feelings of satisfaction for her body may be driven by her perceived deviation from what her race may otherwise suggest.

This internalization of white beauty standards is noteworthy in that it exists outside of interactions with whites. That is, in a social setting made exclusively of Asians, this white-centric hierarchy will still exist. For example, the Korean community at this elite university recognizes a distinction between those who are "international" versus those who are Asian Americans. Amanda, a Korean American first-year student, notes: "I think there's a pressure to avoid international Koreans. I guess I don't want to be labeled as a 'FOB' [fresh off the boat]. I feel that people have negative stereotypes about international Asians and are more accepting of Asian Americans (Asians who have resided in the US for a long time)." Yet we posit it is not the birth location that determines FOB status, but rather ability to uphold white habitus. "International" Koreans are those who are more likely to not have as much English-language capital—manifesting in an unappreciated accent or preference to use a non-English native language. They may lack cultural capital by not dressing in a "suitable style," or lack ability or interest to participate in white-habitus activities such as the pervasive sports culture. In either case, the basis for discrimination is based on white-centric criteria—both when whites discriminate against Asians and when Asians discriminate against themselves.

Adopting Color-blind Ideology to uphold White Habitus

Lastly, Asian Americans in the elite university tend to uphold white habitus by embracing color-blind ideology about Asian Americans in the United States. Though race ideology is not the centerfold of romantic relationships, couples interracial or otherwise constantly navigate social space with racial norms and assumptions. This process of racial navigation is cited as the reason for the decreased length of interracial relationships relative to intraracial ones, and their alternative trajectories of cohabitation suggest interracial couples tend to avoid more public social space.[62] In other words, all relationships form and exist in a space of racial judgment, with certain relationships receiving more social criticism. During the process of racial navigation, "color-blind" ideology denying that Asian Americans are still disadvantaged minorities in America makes for more comfortable interactions with whites. Our data indicate that many respondents tend to embrace certain tenets of "color-blind" ideology relating to the status of Asians in America.

Specifically, Asian Americans students are well aware of Asian economic and educational indicators as well as certain high-profile Asian Americans. However, most focus on this aspect of Asian American status in the United States without any mention of Asian American disadvantage. Karen notes : "I think Asian Americans have made it in the United States judging by the average income of the average household. We are also very influential in the R&D [research-and-development] sector and have definitely made contributions to the American economy." Karen defines making it in America in economic terms; however, her assessment only reflects one part of a bimodal Asian diaspora. While it is true that the median family income of Asian Americans surpasses those of whites, the rate of Asian American poverty also surpasses whites, the indicator of an often-ignored Asian American subpopulation comprising war refugees and poor immigrants typically from Southeast Asia. Karen's failure to acknowledge this population is in line with the white racial frame's depiction of Asian Americans as a model minority: immigrants who have "made it" as a product of their hard work and lack of "racial complaining."

Some students even furthered this idea by suggesting Asian American success was driven by assimilation. This is a common narrative in white-centric color-blind ideology, which suggests that everyone in the United States can do well if they assimilate to the "American" (white) culture.[63] Rauna, an Indian American first-year student, mentions:

> [Asian Americans have] definitely [made it]—I feel like there are some who prefer to only associate with their own race, which is holding them back, but there are many, many more who have mainstreamed into society. I think my parents have made it; I see successful Indian and Asian doctors, lawyers, engineers—prime example, Sanjay Gupta.

Again, there is a focus on professionals in law and in STEM (science, technology, engineering, and math) fields as the pinnacles of success. In addition, Rauna's suggestion for why some Asian Americans are "held back" is that they "prefer to associate with their own race" and forsake opportunities to "mainstream into society." While there is no explicit mention of whites, this prescription for success in America puts the onus on the minority group to accommodate the dominant group of "society," reflecting the hierarchy of social capital that exists to serve whites in America. Asian Americans who use color-blind narratives such as the assimilation theory of success are more likely to gain social capital from white-centric institutions.

Our research also shows some recognition of the structural roadblocks that Asian Americans face, generally involving economic achievement or media attention. The obstacles cited were mostly of relevance to an elite Asian subpopulation. Julie, a Chinese American senior, says this: "While the concept of the bamboo ceiling may exist, many Asian Americans have achieved success nevertheless." The bamboo ceiling (referring mostly to obstacles faced by professionals) and lack of media representation were often cited as areas in which Asian Americans have not yet achieved parity. While these are indeed areas where Asian Americans face obstacles, they are by no means the only areas.

The most disadvantaged Asian American groups were left unmentioned by almost all respondents in the sample. Only one respondent, a Southeast Asian student from a working-class background, mentioned obstacles involving poverty and poor working conditions. Danny, a Vietnamese American sophomore, indicates:

> There's plenty of Asians in the country who just don't have sh*t. These are the ones who operate the small Burmese laundry shops that don't have air conditioning or who wake up at 7 every morning, 365 days a year to go to work in some sh—ty, poorly conditioned building. The worst part is that we're stereotyped to have made it so we don't have any support from other bodies.

Danny's understanding of obstacles facing Asian Americans is very different from his peers—recognizing an often forgotten subpopulation of Asian wage laborers who are lumped together through the model minority stereotype. Danny's interactions with whites in the elite university are shaped through a lens where he understands his racial position relative to theirs. By empathizing with a more harshly oppressed Asian subpopulation, Danny will be more cognizant of anti-Asian "color-blind" framing. Due to the low proportion of Asian students with similar backgrounds (specifically, working-class and Southeast Asian backgrounds), most Asian Americans at the elite university are not aware of aiding the same color-blind ideology that disadvantages Asians as a whole.

The Asian Dating and Marriage Framework

When discussing dating and preparations for marriage, respondents juggled a variety of considerations, including one's own racial considerations, the racial considerations of others, and the personal responsibility of ethnic culture. When put together, they inform an eclectic dating and marriage framework. This frame is constantly undergoing change—especially during students' time in the elite university, where Asians may enter and exit romantic relationships frequently. Especially interesting was respondents' mentions of changes in attraction and romantic involvement over their life course, specifically in the elite university. Further research will be necessary to uncover how the Asian dating and marriage framework is molded over time in cohorts like the one involved in this study.

Students tended to use color-blind language when discussing attraction. Respondents were asked to describe what they look for in potential partners, with race as a suggested characteristic. Responses fell into three coded categories: explicitly color-blind, where the respondent explicitly mentions that race has no bearing; implicitly color-blind, where the respondent does not mention race; and racially selective, where the respondent specifies a preference for a set of racial groups. Responses with reference to the racially specific features "blond hair" and "blue eyes" were coded as white preferential. One respondent expressed a preference for "Hapa" (half white, half Asian) individuals and was coded as racially preferential for both whites and Asians. Most respondents (68 percent) described their potential partners using color-blind language. At face value, this contradicts the findings that most Asian Americans end up with Asian partners, as color-blind preferences (purely random in regards to race) would suggest that more Asians ended up with non-Asian partners. However, this pattern of non-race-preferential attraction and seemingly contradictory intraracial involvement is seen for other racial groups as well, especially whites.[64] The widespread nature of this overall pattern is perhaps a testament to the ubiquity of white habitus informed color-blind ideology, which discourages any overt racial preference, while covertly benefiting whites. The use of explicitly color-blind language is perhaps an indicator of color-blind ideology; however, further research would need to address the reliability of such a claim.

Women in the study were more likely to employ explicitly color-blind or white-seeking racial preference language than men. Of the female respondents, 23 percent used white-seeking language, compared to 14 percent of male respondents. This is the same for explicitly color-blind language (different than white-seeking language); of the female respondents, 23 percent used explicitly color-blind language, compared to 14 percent of male respondents. These results complement the interracial marriage and interracial dating gender patterns among Asian American students: that Asian women tend to out-marry and out-date at a higher rate than their male counterparts. In this case, it is especially interesting to note how explicitly color-blind language and white-seeking language are correlated. This is suggested to be a product of the white-centric language of hegemonic sexuality, which has deracialized whiteness into an invisible "default" race.[65] Thus, language that is "color-blind" is more likely to be white-seeking, simply by the nature of hegemonic sexuality; unracialized, "desirable" characteristics are attributed to whites, leaving a lack of positive language to describe racial minorities without mentioning their race or using derogatory connotations. It is possible respondents who employ more explicitly color-blind language are more well-versed in maintaining white habitus and thus more likely to enter into an interracial relationship. Results complement this theory: 44 percent of respondents who used explicitly color-blind language (explicitly stated no racial preference) entered into interracial relationships with whites at the university, compared to only 25 percent of respondents who used implicitly color-blind language (did not mention a racial preference). If these associations hold true, it marks the concepts of hegemonic sexuality and social exchange theory at work in the language of attraction that Asian Americans use.

Asian Americans are not the sole actors in their romantic lives: Each Asian American student, like every other university student, inhabits a space where their lives and actions are inexplicably tied to the lives and actions of others. In the case of Asian American students, especially women, they are subject to targeting on the basis of their race, a phenomenon we refer to as "yellow targeting." This term comprises both the targeting of Asian American women, commonly referred to as "yellow fever," and the targeting of Asian American men, which is less common and does not have a concrete literature (we will refer to it as "reverse-yellow fever"). At the elite university our respondents attend, we found Asian women more prone to racialized romantic targeting by white men, and Asian men rarely romantically targeted by white women due to race.

Asian American Women and "Yellow Targeting" on Campus

Researchers have documented the specific targeting of Asian and Asian American women by white men in the elite university space.[66]

In previous research at the same elite university, Chou and colleagues found Asian American women to be generally cognizant of their racial fetishization, with some willing to engage in romance with men who racially fetishize them.[67] Most significantly, it was noted that sexualized racist comments about Asian American women were common and ubiquitous, even in the dorm spaces that students call home. It is possible that this is due to the power differential between white men and Asian women in the elite university space—such that white men soliciting women of any color is natural and goes generally unquestioned.[68] Ashley, a Chinese American sophomore, notes that her relationship with a white male drew little notice: "The fact that our relationship is interracial rarely comes up. I think about it more than anyone else, I believe. My parents have never mentioned the fact that [boyfriend] is white as a surprise or shock. My friends (mostly white) have never thought it strange or unnatural either." In a white habitus space the white male–Asian female relationship reinforces the construction of the hegemonically dominant white man.

Some participants who were aware of their fetishization used it to their advantage in constructing an interracial relationship. Ester notes:

> [My sexual partner] said [why he preferred Asians] was because they stay skinnier longer and have better metabolism. They stay more attractive for longer. Though I know he preferred Asians, I don't think he ever exoticized me or treated me differently for being Asian. It was simply a preference for a certain race which I also shared. In that way, we understood each other and were on the same wavelength.

Though she does not mention the racial identity of her sexual partner in this quote, she does mention the possibility of being "exoticized," exotification being understood as an interaction between a white "normal" and a colored "stranger." Later Ester mentions she has only dated white and Asian men, suggesting this partner is white. In her mind, his preference for Asian women was similar to her racial preference for white men, a characteristic they "shared." However, intersectionality scholars suggest this exchange of preferences is not equal—while white men define a hegemonic sexuality, Asian American women are of a subordinated sexuality, meaning they are devalued relative to white men. Thus, the sexuality that defines white men is always dominant, so Asian women are defined in beneficial terms only to be cast as perfect partners for white men.[69] Along these lines, this Asian woman has co-opted her phenotypic capital to enter into an interracial relationship with a white man. Such a transaction of capital was easy for her to perform because it aligned with understood racial and gender structures where white men dominate women and people of color.

"Yellow Fever" Revisited: Emotional Strain

However, not all women in the study were fond of this scenario. Some responded that their interracial relationships were emotionally taxing in a racial sense. Ashley notes that her relationship with her white boyfriend has caused her increasingly more emotional instability:

> I think that my boyfriend might have "yellow fever." I knew at the beginning of our relationship that he was attracted to Asian women more than other kinds of women. This definitely was a red flag, but didn't bother me enough to be a deal breaker. As I've become more ethnically conscious, however, this has started to bother me more and more.

Though her boyfriend's racial affinity to "Asianness" over any other "kind," or characteristic, bothered her from "the beginning," Ashley's discomfort has grown while she has become more "ethnically conscious." This complements the theory of racial double consciousness, which suggests that emotional strain results from conflicting frames. In this case, Ashley's relationship probably reinforced the white racial framing of Asian women as attractive targets for white men, who see them as "racialized others" first, before their other characteristics. Alternatively, being more "ethnically conscious" has probably provided her with a more ethnocentric framing of Asian women as normal and complex, and perhaps she recognizes more the racial targeting and fetishization she is subject to. The combination of both racial fetishization and ethnocentricity causes psychological burden to which only people of color are subject.[70] For women of color, this racial "othering" is only compounded by the "othering" of being a woman.

Exoticized Asian American Men

One male Asian American respondent also mentioned being heterosexually racially targeted. This reverse "yellow fever" is not often recognized, as the trend toward Asian American men is usually racial detraction, not racial attraction. In the sample, we found that the overwhelming majority of respondents either showed depreciation for Asian American men or thought that others depreciated Asian American men. However, Jon, a Chinese senior, notes that he attracts women who have "yellow fever":

> I feel nervous tensions from cultural barriers . . . when speaking with whites. Oddly, I don't feel this at all when speaking to Hispanics or blacks, most likely because these groups also experience oppression, so that is a common trait. I tend to attract women with a bit of "yellow fever" or have a more open-minded global experience from traveling and being well read.

Notice that Jon feels relatively few "cultural barriers" between himself and other people of color who "also experience oppression," unlike whites. Since he does not mention the race of the women he attracts, perhaps this speaks to the different dynamic of reverse yellow fever, whereby Asian American men are targeted by non-Asian women. Intersectionality scholars suggest that it is due to the similar construction of Asian men and other women of color. Specifically, black women have been constructed as sexually undesirable in a hegemonic frame, just as Asian men are.[71] Their similar structural positions allow for some level of connection, though Asian American men still seem to prefer women with similar levels of skin capital. Specifically, Jon has entered into relationships with international students (he mentions a Turkish woman and a Russian woman). This suggests that while he is not dating darker women of color, the women he is involved with are not hegemonically feminine, lacking the cultural capital American-born whites might have. Their unions might be strengthened by the fact that they share subordinate positions on the ladder of hegemonic sexuality.

Conclusion

In this chapter we examined the relationship and dating experiences of Asian American undergraduate students at an elite university using four sociological themes. These themes focused on the co-opting of race during romantic interaction, and are valuable in discussing the navigation of romance through the eyes of an Asian American student at an elite university. While the focus of the themes is macro and structural, the themes play into the individual lives and interactions of Asian students on a micro level. In alignment with prior research, we find that while romance may be explained as an idiosyncratic and highly personalized experience, it is subject to influence from larger structural forces involving race, gender, and their corollary -isms.

While these themes, particularly racial double consciousness, provide a working frame to discuss the narratives of these respondents, only some of them were recognized explicitly. For example, several respondents used ideas of social exchange theory when discussing how white friends "elevated" their social status. Many respondents expressed ideas of intersectionality when they stated that Asian women were stereotyped differently than Asian men. Other ideas, such as the idea of hegemonic sexuality, are not expressed explicitly—most Asian Americans have been socialized into maintaining aspects of white habitus without explicit self-awareness.

In the course of this research, the focus on structural forces has also shed light on the need for additional perspectives on a more micro level. For example, the nuance of familial expectations needs to be explored from a symbolic interactionism perspective beyond our interpretation of it being an expression of capital seeking. Heritage management can be explored in the context of role stress beyond our interpretation of it as racial double consciousness. Most important, we think it is necessary to evaluate how respondents use "talk" to construct their identity and express their desires, beyond using their words to explore their social position. The findings from this chapter can act as a base of understanding for future study on the agency and personal motivations of elite Asian Americans when it comes to their relationship choices.

In the next chapter we explore ways in which our respondents resist racism or are resigned to the racial status quo. We also summarize our findings and discuss their implications, drawing larger conclusions about how race and gender operate in the lives of Asian Americans on college campuses. We also address the areas in need of further research from the implications that have arisen from our analysis. We conclude by addressing the broader implications of our research for understanding US society and for policies that may help lift the weight of everyday racism and sexism. Lastly, we address the areas in need of further research based on implications that arise from our analysis.

Notes

1. Julia Meszaros, "Elliot Rodger and the Effeminization of Asian Men," *Huffington Post*, May 30, 2014. Retrieved from www.huffingtonpost.com/julia-meszaros/elliot-rodger-and-the-effeminization-of-asian-men_b_5401516.html.
2. Amanda Hess, "'If I Can't Have Them, No One Will': How Misogyny Kills Men," *Slate*, May 29, 2014. Retrieved from www.slate.com/blogs/xx_factor/2014/05/29/elliot_rodger_hated_men_because_he_hated_women.html.
3. Meszaros, "Elliot Rodger and the Effeminization of Asian Men."
4. Rosalind S. Chou, *Asian American Sexual Politics: The Construction of Race, Gender, and Sexuality* (Lanham, MD: Rowman and Littlefield, 2012).
5. Linda M. Burton and C. R. Hardaway, "Low-Income Mothers as 'Othermothers' to Their Romantic Partners' Children," *Family Process* 51 (2012): 343–359.
6. Milton Gordon, *Assimilation in American Life: The Role of Race, Religion, and National Origins* (Oxford: Oxford University Press, 1964).
7. Robert T. Teranishi, *Asians in the Ivory Tower: Dilemmas of Racial Inequality in American Higher Education* (New York: Teachers College Press, 2010).
8. US Census, 2006.
9. US Census, 1960 and 1970.
10. Sharon Lee and Marilyn Fernandez, "Trends in Asian American Racial/Ethnic Intermarriage: A Comparison of 1980 and 1990 Census Data," *Sociological Perspectives* 41, no. 2 (1998): 323–342.
11. S. Sassler and K. Joyner, "Social Exchange and the Progression of Sexual Relationships in Emerging Adulthood," *Social Forces* 90, no. 1 (2011): 223–245.
12. Chou, *Asian American Sexual Politics*.
13. US Census, 2006.
14. Ibid.
15. Frank Wu, *Yellow: Race in America beyond Black and White* (New Haven, CT: Yale University Press, 2003).
16. Ibid.
17. Eduardo Bonilla-Silva, "From Bi-racial to Tri-racial: Towards a New System of Racial Stratification in the USA," *Ethnic and Racial Studies* 27, no. 6 (2004): 931–950.
18. Andrew Kohut, "The Rise of Asian Americans," Pew Research Center, 2012.
19. Lee and Fernandez, "Trends in Asian American Racial/Ethnic Intermarriage."
20. Paul Taylor, "Marrying Out," Pew Research Center, 2010.
21. Ronald Takaki, *Strangers from a Different Shore* (Boston: Back Bay, 1998).
22. Harry H. Kitano, *Asian Americans: Emerging Minorities* (New York: Prentice Hall, 2004).
23. US Census, 2006.
24. Chou, *Asian American Sexual Politics*.
25. Kingsley Davis, "Intermarriage in Caste Societies," *American Anthropologist* 43, no. 3 (1941): 376–395.
26. Roy F. Baumeister and Kathleen D. Vohs, "Sexual Economics: Sex as Female Resource for Social Exchange in Heterosexual Interactions," *Personality and Social Psychology Review* 8, no. 4 (2004): 339–363.

27. Sassler and Joyner, "Social Exchange and the Progression of Sexual Relationships in Emerging Adulthood."
28. Pierre Bourdieu, "The Forms of Capital," *Handbook of Theory and Research for the Sociology of Education* (New York: Greenwood, 1986).
29. Chou, *Asian American Sexual Politics*.
30. Joe R. Feagin, *The White Racial Frame: Centuries of Racial Framing and Counter-Framing* (New York: Routledge, 2009).
31. Stanley Gaines and William Ickes, "Perspectives on Interracial Relationships," in *Handbook of Personal Relationships: Theory, Research, and Interventions*, 2nd ed., 197–220. 1997.
32. Michael Rosenfeld, "A Critique of Exchange Theory in Mate Selection," *American Journal of Sociology* 110 no. 5 (2005): 1284–1325.
33. R.W. Connell and James Messerschmidt, "Hegemonic Masculinity: Rethinking the Concept," *Gender and Society* 19, no. 6 (2005): 845–854.
34. Bonilla-Silva, "From Bi-racial to Tri-racial."
35. Wendy Moore, *Reproducing Racism* (Lanham, MD: Rowman and Littlefield, 2008).
36. Rosalind S. Chou, Kristen Lee, and Simon Ho, "The White Habitus and Hegemonic Masculinity at the Elite Southern University: Asian Americans and the Need for Intersectional Analysis," *Sociation Today* 10, no. 2 (2012).
37. Ibid.
38. William Edward Du Bois, *The Souls of Black Folks* (Chicago: A.C. McClurg, 1903), 186–187.
39. Meghan Burke, "Discursive Fault Lines: Reproducing White Habitus in a Racially Diverse Community," *Critical Sociology* (2012): 645–668.
40. Chou, Lee, and Ho, "The White Habitus and Hegemonic Masculinity at the Elite Southern University."
41. Ibid.
42. Patricia Hill Collins, *Black Sexual Politics* (New York: Routledge, 2004).
43. Ibid.
44. Chou and Feagin, *The Myth of the Model Minority*.
45. Yen Le Espiritu, *Asian American Women and Men: Labor, Laws, and Love* (Lanham, MD: Rowman and Littlefield, 2008).
46. Elaine Kim, "'Such Opposite Creatures': Men and Women in Asian American Literature," *Michigan Quarterly Review* 29, no. 70 (1990).
47. David Eng, *Racial Castration: Managing Masculinity in Asian America (Perverse Modernities)* (Durham, NC: Duke University Press, 2001).
48. Kim, "Such Opposite Creatures."
49. Collins, *Black Sexual Politics*.
50. Chou, *Asian American Sexual Politics*.
51. Feagin, *The White Racial Frame*.
52. Espiritu, *Asian American Women and Men*.
53. Chou, *Asian American Sexual Politics*.
54. Chou and Feagin, *The Myth of the Model Minority*.
55. Kitano, *Asian American*.
56. Ibid.
57. Elizabeth A. Armstrong, "Sexual Assault on Campus: A Multi-Level Integrative Approach to Party Rape," *Social Problems* 53 (2006): 483–499.
58. Moore, *Reproducing Racism*.
59. Armstrong, "Sexual Assault on Campus."
60. S.R. Harper and S.J. Quaye, "Student Organizations as Venues for Black Identity Expression and Development among African American Male Student Leaders," *Journal of College Student Development* 48 (2007): 127–144.

61. Chou, Lee, and Ho, "The White Habitus and Hegemonic Masculinity at the Elite Southern University."
62. Sassler and Joyner, "Social Exchange and the Progression of Sexual Relationships in Emerging Adulthood."
63. Amanda E. Lewis, M. Chesler, and Tyrone A. Forman, "The Impact of 'Colorblind' Ideologies on Students of Color: Intergroup Relations at a Predominantly White University," *Journal of Negro Education* 69 (2000): 74–91.
64. Eduardo Bonilla-Silva, *Racism without Racists: Color-Blind Racism and the Persistence of Racial Inequality in the United States* (Lanham, MD: Rowman and Littlefield, 2010).
65. Collins, *Black Sexual Politics*.
66. Wu, *Yellow*.
67. Chou, Lee, and Ho, "The White Habitus and Hegemonic Masculinity at the Elite Southern University."
68. R. Ray and J. A. Rosow, "Getting Off and Getting Intimate: How Normative Institutional Arrangements Structure Black and White Fraternity Men's Approaches toward Women," *Men and Masculinities* 12, no. 5 (August 2010): 523–546.
69. Kim, "Such Opposite Creatures."
70. Chou and Feagin, *The Myth of the Model Minority*.
71. Collins, *Black Sexual Politics*.

5
CONCLUSION
Resign or Resist? Disengage or Engage?

Introduction

In early spring 2011 a young white college student named Alexandra Wallace posted a video on YouTube causing a nationwide uproar. In what she titled "Asians in the Library," Wallace chastises the "hordes of Asians" at the University of California–Los Angeles for not having "American" manners and their parents for "not teaching their kids to fend for themselves." She also makes a mockery of Asians who speak their native languages: "Ohh Ching chong ling long ting tong? Ohh."[1] Under heavy public criticism in response to the video, Wallace eventually resigned from UCLA. She received no institutional punishment for her racist statements, and according to UCLA's official press release on the subject, Wallace's video did not violate the student code, nor did it "seek to harm or threaten a specific person or group."[2] What is even more remarkable is that Wallace enjoyed some fame—she was invited to MTV's Jersey Shore reunion show, and has been featured in a co-ed magazine bikini photo shoot as the "UCLA Asian Racist."[3]

Although Alexandra Wallace's is one of the more extreme cases of racial hostility to occur in recent years, it provides an opportunity to examine both the acceptability of racism against Asian Americans and white normative university politics. By failing to pursue action against Alexandra Wallace, UCLA administrators prioritized a single white student's right to anti-Asian racist bombast as a matter of free speech over the right of their Asian American students to operate within a tolerant community. More alarming, UCLA's statement that the video did not "seek to harm or threaten a specific person or group" minimized the emotional destruction its Asian American students experience as a consequence of racism. By reframing the discussion around the "intentionality" of Alexandra Wallace's video, UCLA attempted to excuse the racism embedded throughout her diatribe. Unfortunately this is not an isolated situation of clueless administrators but rather an example of how white social institutions founded on racial inequalities continue to operate within a white normative frame that allows racism to persist. Moreover, that Alexandra Wallace gained celebrity from her racist tirade further underlines how the use of Asian Americans as a punch line is still profitable in mainstream white American culture.

The Wallace incident at UCLA also shows us that white institutional space trumps other factors. UCLA's undergraduate makeup as of the 2013 fall quarter was 34.8 percent Asian/Pacific Islander, 3.8 percent African American, 18 percent Hispanic, and 27.8 percent white. These numbers do not include the 11.8 percent of international students, of which a portion is from Asian countries. While Asian and Pacific Islander students are the majority at this elite private West Coast institution (which is often portrayed as Asian-friendly), white institutional space dictates the racial climate. Numerous racist incidents at UCLA have made headlines in recent years, including a lawsuit brought by an African American professor in the school of medicine against his own department, a black law student receiving hate mail, and anti-Asian flyers posted across campus in both 2012 and 2014.[4] We challenge the argument that diverse representation can effectively combat racism. White institutional space must be critically examined and challenged before racial oppression can be dismantled.

In this chapter we present ways in which our Asian American participants dealt with the racial climate at their university. We classify their reactions in two ways—*resignation* or *resistance*. Individuals were not inclined to exclusively resign or exclusively resist; positionality and location mattered. However, we aim to highlight that there is a spectrum of ways in which our respondents responded to racism. Additionally, we asked our participants to give advice to other Asian Americans who may be dealing with similar situations, and we organized their responses into two categories. We found that advice either suggested *racial disengagement* or *racial engagement*, two opposing types of suggestions. Finally, we offer a summary of our research, their implications, and suggestions for future areas in need of research.

Resignation v. Resistance

Asian Americans in college seem to suffer from many racialized social experiences that shape how they live and navigate their daily lives. As elucidated above, these experiences are often intersectional, gendered, and raced. Many problems are complex and involve various social and personal pressures. Asian American students are continually faced with the question of how to react to these problems on a day-to-day basis. While there are many different ways Asian Americans have chosen to respond to these problems, navigating the white-dominated space of college universities requires significant emotional management on the part of its students of color, regardless of how they choose to react. To illustrate a dichotomy in responses, the way they deal with these problems has been grouped into two strands: resignation and resistance.

Resignation

Resistance and resignation are not mutually exclusive responses to racism. Asian Americans students responding via resignation direct their behavior and responses toward fitting into white space in an attempt to make it a safe space for them. They use resignation to affirm notions of Asian Americans as irregular and whites as normal. Growing up in the South, among a population with a majority of middle-class whites, Ted talks about his perspectives on facing social problems as an Asian American:

> To an extent, I believe it's very overcomable [*sic*], if you're an Asian American with the right personality, the right character. I guess height always works in the business world. I would say

that the generalizations always comes from the fact that so many Asians falling under the stereotype. So we're obviously disadvantaged, but it's very overcomable [sic] if you're the right type of person.

Ted recognizes a disadvantage to being Asian American in a white-dominated world. He talks about "overcoming" difficulties through having a certain set of characteristics. By mentioning being disadvantaged by "generalizations" stemming from other Asian Americans "falling under the stereotype," Ted has shifted the blame for his difficulties fitting into a white society onto other Asian Americans.

With the creation of favorable racial social spaces, the strength of color-blindness elicits negative reactions from Asian Americans. When asked about how Asian Americans interact in social spaces Kate, a Korean American female senior, says:

So if someone takes [Asian American stereotypes] to heart, which they definitely can, it will make them less confident socially and more self-aware, more socially awkward, maybe less willing to engage with those different from them so maybe that would lead to them being more secluded and more self-segregated, like hanging out with only Asians.

By using the term *self-segregated*, Kate has internalized the language of white privilege and color-blindness. Using this term to accuse people of color of being exclusionary and to stigmatize minority social spaces is characteristic of color-blind discourse utilized by whites. Kate fails to articulate how having Asian American friends and being a part of a racial minority group could be a protective choice against the difficulties of white-dominant university spaces and stereotyping. Despite the best resistance efforts, color-blindness and hegemonic ideology can still seep into Asian American perspective.

Respondents also pointed to ignoring discrimination and racism as an effective way to deal with unwanted comments. When asked whether he has experienced any comments on his race, Richard, an Asian American male senior, says, "Yes, the common joke is that Asians have small penises. It obviously is very degrading and embarrassing, but I've never really paid attention to that type of bigotry." Moreover, when asked about advice for Asian Americans struggling with racism, Paul, a Asian American male first-year student, replies, "Even if they are being judged, they should ignore the discriminators and move on and/or have a third party intervene to reduce conflict." The advice here appears counter to the earlier advice about support in numbers that Paul offered. Erika, a Chinese American female senior, says when asked if she experienced racism, "Yes, it's something that I usually just ignore and don't think about. Sometimes it'll really make me sad/angry . . . but I've never actually done anything about it before." While it is important to ask for resources and help when things are overwhelming, it also requires a great deal of emotional management to ignore racism.

From the interview responses it seems Asian American undergraduates are divided between resistance and resignation as their principal strategies for coping with racism. In both cases, Asian Americans must perform emotional work to cope with these racialized experiences at historically white colleges and universities.

Resistance

To resist the white racial frame of institutional space and oppressive racial ideologies, whites and people of color use "counter frames."[5] Many Asian American students who grew up in more racially heterogeneous communities were surprised to find that the social scenes in our Southern elite university were divided along racial lines—this despite an undergraduate student body that is around 40 percent people of color. The socialization process, which we argue is "white habitus," at college informs students' romantic, social, and racialized life. Particularly the role that individuals play in the university culture is heavily dependent on their affiliation with the (historically white) Greek system. Tim, an Asian American junior, talks about his experience with the campus nightlife:

> I can't really say it [the historically white Greek system] hasn't affected me because you go to the quad and you have white fraternities living there and they're the ones who have the parties,

they're the ones who host things. So, it's really hard to not be affected by it on some level.

For many Asian Americans and other students of color the historically white Greek system seems to be the heart of the university nightlife, and as Tim mentions, "it's hard to not be affected by it on some level." Asian Americans who respond via resistance recognize the difficulties in being Asian American in a white-dominated space. Their responses are directed at creating space that is safe for them, and acknowledgement of the Asian American identity as worthy.

Many of the students we interviewed said that they had close Asian American friends. Generally, Asian Americans chose other Asian Americans to befriend because they have lived through common racial experience. Having Asian American friends appears important to coping with and resisting racialized experiences. When asked, "For Asian Americans struggling with racism and their identity, what advice would you give them?" Paul, a first-year Asian American student, wrote:

> As cultural historian Xiaoqun Xu has said, "Discourse is power." Asian Americans struggling with racism and their identity should find people who they are comfortable with talking about their struggle. I for one would be glad to listen to what they have to say and make short responses and comments on my opinions.

Common racialized experiences allow people of color to validate each other's struggles to deal with everyday racism rather than negating them through color-blindness. Janine, a Chinese American junior, also touches upon the struggle to combat color-blindness in her advice to those combating racism:

> Seek other people out. It is really comforting to hear other people affirm what you feel, so don't stop until you find someone who agrees with you, and whatever you're feeling is right; and then you can talk to that person about your troubles. It is really comforting to know that you are not crazy.

Janine advises those experiencing racism to find people who will affirm rather than dismiss those racialized experiences. In color-blind racism, the racialized experience is negated and the person experiencing racism is meant to feel crazy, irrational, or paranoid, and is less likely to speak out again. Janine's advice to have friends who affirm racism is a small but important step to building resistance against color-blind racism.

Moreover, respondents spoke of Asian American undergraduate social organizations constructed in a way that resists stereotypical images by painting the opposite picture. Ted speaks of the counter-imaging in his Asian American fraternity:

> Our motto is, "to be leaders among men." But not everyone tries to be a leader, that's just our motto. I guess our image is Asian guys who, you know, are sociable, who can throw down."

The Asian American fraternity is bound by a formal motto as well as a more common image that its members "are sociable" and "can throw down." The desirable portrayal of Asian Americans as social leaders is a denial of stereotypical representations of Asian American males as quiet, socially awkward nerds who can't lead. This particular Asian American group attempts to redefine its members and what it means to be Asian American.

Counter-Narratives

The white racial frame is a concept that racial ideology is held consciously and unconsciously by most white Americans and by many people of color—including racial imagery, emotions, and narratives that shape their understanding of race and their behavior.[6] Creating a different racial perspective has been paramount for the development of African American support for racialized experiences. Asian Americans have also begun to develop a different "frame" by understanding how race shapes interactions in America from their perspective. This counter-frame aids people of color by helping them notice and make sense of their racialized experiences. Wade, a Chinese American first-year student, shares how his parents explained to him the merits of academic achievement. Like some Asian Americans families, there is a fear that affirmative action works to the detriment of Asian Americans and unfairly rewards other people of color:

> [My parents] kept highlighting the fact that because you're Asian, it's more difficult for you to get into schools, so you need to do better. Also because my school was majority Asian, they were like, "You can already compare yourself with your peers, because your school is simply Asian, and because you're Asian yourself, you will be judged by higher standards, so you'll have to work harder."

This kind of conversation seems common among Asian American students, as affirmative action has become a racialized concept that is present in many middle-class Asian American homes. Noticing and recognizing that one will be treated differently based on race is an essential part of a successful counter-frame. It is unfortunate that the topic of affirmative action as part of the Asian American counter-frame may breed competition and seeds of distrust among the members of the Asian American community; however, it is still a valuable common perspective that brings the community somewhat closer together in terms of a collective racial consciousness.

Another critically important aspect of a racial counter-frame is identifying the way in which society's structure favors whites. In response to the question, "For Asian Americans struggling with racism and their identity, what advice would you give them?", Beth, a Chinese American sophomore, says:

> Don't give a shit about what white people think you are supposed to do. Asians are not "supposed" to do anything. We operate with all the same rights, freedoms, desires, fears, sexual urges, despair, [and] anger as white people—and, yes, even in dating and hooking up. You can have as much sex or as little sex or no sex with whomever you want. Asian women are just as beautiful as white women. Asian men are just as sexy as white men. Believe it, live it.

This respondent recognizes and rejects Asian American racial boundaries that white ideology has created and attempts to remove expectations on sexualized racism and beauty. Her counter-narrative attempts to free Asian Americans from subordination to whites by recognizing that Asian Americans' rights, emotions, and desires have value.

Racial Disengagement and Racial Engagement

As Asian Americans move into adulthood and possibly start their transition into marriage and parenthood, they are burdened by the choice of upholding family heritage. While some Asian Americans are ready to "move beyond" their racial identity, others recognize it as an unalienable part of their identity that must be embraced. The respondents in our study were asked what advice they would give to other Asian Americans dealing with racism and identity issues. The advice tended to fall into two groups: one that suggested indifference to the concerns of others—we call this *racial disengagement*—and another that suggested actively coming to terms with the pressures of racial identity, which we will call *racial engagement*. In this sample, we found that those who use racially explicit language of attraction are more likely to suggest racial engagement. Most male respondents (60 percent) suggested racial engagement compared to racial disengagement (40 percent). Women were equally likely to suggest racial engagement (52 percent) as racial disengagement (48 percent). These results may be a product of the hierarchy of hegemonic sexuality—white-centric hegemonic sexuality deemphasizes race, thus those closer to hegemonic sexuality should be less racially engaged.

Racial Disengagement

Racial disengagement takes on a language similar to color-blind ideology and is rooted in the idea that "everyone can be who they want to" with no consideration to obstacles. Racial disengagement is about keeping your chin up and "not caring what others think." Though semantically different, it follows the stereotypical view of model minority racial politics, which is to "keep your head down" and "don't rock the boat"; neither of these actions suggests actively engaging with race as a concept larger than a personal identity. Anne, a Chinese American senior, suggests to others to just move beyond race: "Just accept that you are an Asian American but that doesn't really define who you are. What really defines you is what you do, what you like, etc. You don't need to fit neatly into a category that people have created based on your race." While this advice seems both accepting of one's racial identity and "beyond" categorization and stereotyping, it too easily falls into the "postracial" narrative of color-blind ideology—namely that in America, racial differences do not matter (or at least, do not need to matter) in one's life.

As Bonilla-Silva argues, this narrative is a commonly used tool by whites, especially "liberal" whites, to maintain white centrality while not seeming "racist." By suggesting that race matters, but not to a point where it "has to matter" in one's life, this narrative ironically makes the opposite claim: that we are beyond race. If race only matters "by choice," then it really does not matter. By extrapolation, if race does not matter, then neither does racial discrimination, or other structural barriers against people of color. If race need not matter, people of color are to blame for their own position "at the bottom of the well."[7] Asian Americans and Jewish Americans are perfect accomplices in this ruse, as both groups were historically disadvantaged but have risen in certain economic indicators to the point where they are at parity with whites in general. Too often, emigrants of color—especially Asian Americans—will promote the narrative of "race not having to matter," because as history has shown, "keeping one's head down" and "not rocking the boat" have resulted in economic parity with whites. This is at the root of the model minority concept: the way some light-skinned East Asians co-opt the color-blind narrative of "race not having to matter" to compound the white privilege they already gain from their phenotypic capital.

Racial Engagement

Not all Asian Americans are as fast to distance themselves from race, and many of our respondents suggested that their racial identity was an inescapable facet of their lives. These respondents were proponents of racial engagement: the time and effort necessary in coming to terms with one's identity as a person of color. The language of racial engagement is less positive and focuses on obstacles. Though it does allow for the openness of possibilities, it stresses the role of race and culture in every possibility. Tim says:

> Never ever forget who you are and where you came from. Never ever allow yourself to denigrate your own upbringing and your

own cultural identity. Even if you don't really associate with Asian Americans or with your expected "identity," never feel afraid to approach Asian Americans who are more representative of traditional viewpoints.

Tim's statement allows for the possibility of "nonassociation" with other Asian Americans. However, the thing he expressly discourages is "forgetting" one's upbringing and racial identity: "who you are." Tim's statement makes sense assuming a society where racial discrimination is recognized and permanent. If one's own race is consistently a factor of consideration to others who hold decision-making powers, then it will forever be an inalienable factor in one's life. In this scenario, the ability to "be at peace" with one's race and culture means being able to cope with the double consciousness of being racialized, and holding racial identity.

These two patterns of heritage management suggest two different ideologies within the Asian American community. Some see the world through two lenses, one that operates on the "front stage" according to the rules of white habitus and color-blind ideology, and the second, which pays attention to what happens "behind the veil," where race and culture do not only matter but are elementary to the proceedings of everyday life. Those individuals are more likely to see race as inescapable, and suggest racial engagement. This is perhaps why racial engagers are also more likely to explain attraction racially. They are more likely to see themselves as outsiders and believe that others see them as the same, reinforcing their "behind the veil" lens of racial social operation. Perhaps this is why more racial engagers are men: the construction of Asian men has been more sexually alienating than that of Asian American women.

Conclusion

I, Rosalind Chou, have been giving lectures and speeches about Asian Americans and racism in the United States since 2007. The crowds have varied from five to 500 people, and at the conclusion of each talk I am asked the same question, like clockwork. A hopeful attendee always asks, "What do we do to stop racism in the United States?" As a social scientist trained in data collection and analysis, I am always a bit uncomfortable answering this question. I am typically more interested in the theoretical questions for which my data collection can exact some sort of trend. I am not often called upon to solve such social problems with my tape recorder and transcriptions.

Do I think Asian Americans are fully respected and accepted as equal citizens in the United States? If that were the case then we would not have been be so publicly humiliated in recent years by the likes of Rosie O'Donnell, Rush Limbaugh, and Alexandra Wallace as they mocked Asian language, just as many non-Asian children are doing on school playgrounds across the nation.

Social scientists are often trained to distance themselves from emotions. It is something we have to do to be "objective," yet this type of mindset is central to supporting white supremacy.[8] In both undergraduate and graduate training, the knowledge factories (HWCUs) are white institutionalized space. There is, as Wendy Moore theorizes,[9] (1) racist exclusion of people of color from positions of power in the institution. While some universities now have people of color in the upper echelons of leadership, they are still too few. The HWCUs then (2) develop a white frame that organizes the logic of the institution; this can be seen in the admissions policies, hierarchy of organizations on campus, faculty makeup, and so on, which goes unquestioned and seen as normal.

Then the curriculum at these white institutions is (3) a historical construction of a curricular model based upon the thinking of white elites. Students of color may find it hard to take a class with counter-narratives or counter-frames. These students are told to be emotionless when talking about past historical atrocities, and that scientific and objective minds are ideal. Yet emotional management is a key component to racial oppression. Whites hold the power to define racism, dictate when people of color can be outraged, and enforce or ignore incidents on campus. This last component of white institutional space is mystifying the whole process with (4) the assertion that university policies are a neutral and impartial body of doctrine unconnected to power relations. We see this at universities especially concerning affirmative action versus legacy policies. While affirmative action policies have basically been struck down at universities nationwide, legacy policies remain. Affirmative action has wrongly been rendered racial preference for unqualified students of color, but legacy policies that benefit white students (because of the historical exclusion of people of color at HWCUs) appear to be unconnected to racism and white power. It is through these four elements that white institutional space developed and why it still persists.

So, we encourage further *critical* research that puts issues in *historical context*. Just getting into college does not change white institutional space. More research that can incorporate standpoint epistemology, a bottom-up perspective, will give rise to alternatives to the white-dominated curriculum. Students could put pressure on their administrations for more course offerings, majors, and student services related to race and racism in the United States.

As colleges and universities face scrutiny for their rape policies, most administrations put the onus on students to change the climate. Additionally, they hope that students' finite time on campus, with turnover every four to five years, will keep any major institutional change at bay.[10] We see the same issues arise for student groups that get wind in their sails fighting a racially hostile campus climate. Alumni groups must remain involved to gain consistency and real traction for racial progression at colleges and universities.

On a personal level, if Asian Americans are seen as racial others in a white supremacist society, then the next question is, what are we going to do about it? Sometimes I feel like I have a great burden on my shoulders. I have actually had a friend tell me that the weight of all Asian Americans rests upon them. Why? It is because I'm critical of the racial status quo and I attempt to counter the white racial frame. These notions make me an outlier. Some of us may be comfortable with middle-class crumbs and seemingly "positive" stereotypes, but I'd rather have freedom: freedom from racist taunting, freedom from demeaning media constructions, and freedom to define my identity without assumptions about my race, gender, sexuality, mind, body, and spirit.

At times, I confront people to their faces. When I mention this at my lectures or talks, what I find, every time, is that there are Asian Americans in the audience that relate. They come up to me after the talk, thanking me for telling their stories and standing up for them.

As dedicated as I am to the cause, as are Kristen and Simon, we cannot do this by ourselves. We need your help. At the very personal level, in your own life, you control your own actions and your own fate. You can stand up for yourself. This is not necessarily a call for you to be a new civil rights leader, to start a movement. We urge you to take care of yourself, honor yourself as an individual by learning to fight and to stand up for yourself, to be able to demand respect from others when they do not treat you with dignity. The very first step is deconstructing the external messages about whom you are supposed to be based on your socio-historically constructed race, gender, and sexuality. We are not what they say we are. We are who we want to be. By decolonizing your mind, you can begin to live free.

After recognizing racist, sexist, and homophobic constructions, you can take the next step, finding your voice. As an Asian American I have been publicly ridiculed a number of times, and in my rage I have found myself speechless and paralyzed. I have overcome the fear and now have allowed myself to speak—to yell, in fact, and to scream. I know that no one else is going to do it for me. Now it's your turn.

Notes

1. Alexander Wallace, "Asians in the Library," last modified March 2011, www.youtube.com.
2. Associated Press, "Alexandra Wallace, Student in Anti-Asian Rant, Says She'll Leave UCLA," *Huffington Post*, March 19, 2011, www.huffingtonpost.com.
3. "Meet Alexandra Wallace: The UCLA Ranting Racist," *Co-ed Magazine*, March 14, 2011, http://coedmagazine.com.
4. Dennis Romero, "Racist, Anti-Asian Flier Rocks UCLA, USC Campuses." *LA Blogs*, 2014, www.laweekly.com/informer/2014/02/11/racist-anti-asian-flier-rocks-ucla-usc-campuses 2014.
5. Rosalind S. Chou, *Asian American Sexual Politics: The Construction of Race, Gender, and Sexuality* (Lanham, MD: Rowman and Littlefield, 2012); Joe R. Feagin, *The White Racial Frame: Centuries of Racial Framing and Counter-Framing* (New York: Routledge, 2009).
6. Feagin, *The White Racial Frame*.
7. Eduardo Bonilla-Silva, *Racism without Racists: Color-Blind Racism and the Persistence of Racial Inequality in the United States* (Lanham, MD: Rowman and Littlefield, 2006).
8. Wendy L. Moore, *Reproducing Racism: White Space, Elite Law Schools, and Racial Inequality* (Lanham, MD: Rowman and Littlefield, 2008).
9. Ibid.
10. Jennifer Ludden, "Student Activists Keep Pressure on Campus Sexual Assault." *NPR*, 2014, www.npr.org/2014/08/26/343352075/student-activists-keep-sexual-assault-issues-in-the-spotlight.

REFERENCES

Armstrong, Elizabeth A. 2006. "Sexual Assault on Campus: A Multi-Level Integrative Approach to Party Rape." *Social Problems* 53: 483–499.
"Asian Sex Movies." 2011. *Redtube*. www.redtube.com.
Associated Press. 2011. "Alexandra Wallace, Student in Anti-Asian Rant, Says She'll Leave UCLA." *Huffington Post*. www.huffingtonpost.com/2011/03/19/alexandra-wallace-student_n_837925.html.
Baumeister, Roy F., and Kathleen D. Vohs. 2004. "Sexual Economics: Sex as Female Resource for Social Exchange in Heterosexual Interactions." *Personality and Social Psychology Review* 8(4): 339–63.
Bonilla-Silva, Eduardo. 1997. "Rethinking Racism: Toward a Structural Interpretation." *American Sociological Review* 62(3): 465–480.
———. 2002. "The Linguistics of Color Blind Racism: How to Talk Nasty about Blacks without Sounding 'Racist.'" *Critical Sociology* 28(1): 41–64.
———. 2004. "From Bi-racial to Tri-racial: Towards a New System of Racial Stratification in the USA." *Ethnic and Racial Studies* 27(6).
———. 2006. *Racism without Racists: Color-Blind Racism and the Persistence of Racial Inequality in the United States*. Lanham, MD: Rowman and Littlefield.
———. 2012. "The Invisible Weight of Whiteness: the Racial Grammar of Everyday Life in Contemporary America." *Ethnic and Racial Studies* 35(2): 183–185.
Bonilla-Silva, Eduardo, and David G. Embrick. 2007. "'Every Place Has a Ghetto...': The Significance of Whites' Social and Residential Segregation." *Journal of Symbolic Interaction* 30(3): 323–346.
Bourdieu, Pierre P. 1986. "The Forms of Capital." *Handbook of Theory and Research for the Sociology of Education*. New York: Greenwood.
Burawoy, Michael. 1998. "The Extended Case Method." In *Ethnography Unbound*, edited by M. Burawoy, A. Burton, A.A. Ferguson, K.J. Fox, J. Gamson, N. Gartrell, L. Hurst, C. Kurzman, L. Salzinger, J. Schiffman, and S. Ui. Berkeley: University of California Press.
Burke, Meghan. 2012. "Discursive Fault Lines: Reproducing White Habitus in a Racially Diverse Community." *Critical Sociology*.
Burton, Linda M., and C.R. Hardaway. 2012. "Low-Income Mothers as 'Othermothers' to Their Romantic Partners' Children." *Family Process* 51: 343–359.

Chang, M.J. 2011. "Battle Hymn of the Model Minority Myth." *Amerasia Journal* 37(2): 137–143.
Chou, Rosalind S. 2012. *Asian American Sexual Politics: The Construction of Race, Gender, and Sexuality*. Lanham, MD: Rowman and Littlefield.
Chou, Rosalind S., and Joe R. Feagin. 2008. (Second edition 2014). *The Myth of the Model Minority: Asian Americans Facing Racism*. Boulder, CO: Paradigm.
Chou, Rosalind S., Kristen Lee, and Simon Ho. 2012. "The White Habitus and Hegemonic Masculinity at the Elite Southern University: Asian Americans and the Need for Intersectional Analysis." *Sociation Today* 10(2).
Chu, Ying. 2009. "The New Trophy Wives: Asian Women." *Marie Claire*. www.marieclaire.com/sex-love/advice/asian-trophy-wife.
Chua, Amy. 2011a. *Battle Hymn of the Tiger Mother*. New York: Penguin.
Chua, Amy. 2011b. "Why Chinese Mothers Are Superior." *Wall Street Journal*. http://online.wsj.com.
Clark, Kim. 2009. "Do Elite Private Colleges Discriminate against Asian Students?" *US News*. www.usnews.com.
Collins, Patricia Hill. 2004. *Black Sexual Politics*. New York: Routledge.
Connell, R.W., and James Messerschmidt. 2005. "Hegemonic Masculinity: Rethinking the Concept." *Gender and Society* 19(6): 845–854.
Davis, Kingsley. 1941. "Intermarriage in Caste Societies." *American Anthropologist* 43(3): 376–395.
De Graaf, Mia. 2014. "Uni of Alabama All-White Sororities Win Right to Remain Racist after Rejecting Two Applicants for Being Black." *Mail Online*. www.dailymail.co.uk/news/article-2588883/Uni-Alabama-white-sororities-win-right-remain-racist-rejecting-two-applicants-black.html.
Du Bois, William Edward. 1903. *The Souls of Black Folks*. Chicago: A.C. McClurg.
Eng, David. 2001. *Racial Castration: Managing Masculinity in Asian America (Perverse Modernities)*. Durham, NC: Duke University Press.
Espiritu, Yen Le. 2008. *Asian American Women and Men: Labor, Laws, and Love*. Lanham, MD: Rowman and Littlefield.
Feagin, Joe R. 2002. "The Continuing Significance of Racism: US Colleges and Universities." *American Council on Education. Office of Minorities in Higher Education* 1(4): 1–54.
———. 2009. *The White Racial Frame: Centuries of Racial Framing and Counter-Framing*. New York: Routledge.
———. 2014. *Racist America: Roots, Current Realities, and Future Reparations*. New York: Routledge.
Feagin, Joe R. and Karyn D. McKinney. 2003. *The Many Costs of Racism*. Lanham, MD: Rowman and Littlefield.
Gaines, Stanley, and William Ickes. 1996. "Perspectives on Interracial Relationships." In *Handbook of Personal Relationships: Theory, Research, and Interventions*, edited by Steve Duck, 197–220. Hoboken, NJ: Wiley.
Gordon, Milton. 1964. *Assimilation in American Life: The Role of Race, Religion, and National Origins*. Oxford: Oxford University Press.
Grier, William H., and Price M. Cobbs. 1968. *Black Rage*. New York: Bantam.
Guiffrida, D.A. 2003. "African American Student Organizations as Agents of Social Integration." *Journal of College Student Development* 44: 304–319.
Harper, S.R., and S.J. Quaye. 2007. "Student Organizations as Venues for Black Identity Expression and Development among African American Male Student Leaders." *Journal of College Student Development* 48: 127–144.
Heldman, Caroline, and Danielle Dirks. 2014. "Blowing the Whistle on Campus Rape." *Ms. Magazine* 24(1).

REFERENCES

Hess, Amanda. 2014. "'If I Can't Have Them, No One Will': How Misogyny Kills Men." *Slate*. www.slate.com/blogs/xx_factor/2014/05/29/elliot_rodger_hated_men_because_he_hated_women.html.

Jaschik, Scott. 2014. "Snow Hate: A Tale of Two Chancellors." *Inside Higher Ed*. www.insidehighered.com/news/2014/01/28/u-illinois-decision-keep-classes-going-leads-racist-and-sexist-twitter-attacks.

Kardiner, Abraham, and Lionel Ovesey. 1962. *The Mark of Oppression: Explorations in the Personality of the American Negro*. Cleveland: World Publishing Company.

Keith, Verna M., Karen Lincoln, Robert J. Taylor, and James S. Jackson. "Discriminatory Experiences and Depressive Symptoms among African American Women: Do Skin Tone and Mastery Matter?" *Sex Roles* 62: 48–59.

Kim, B. 2011. "Asian Female and Caucasian Male Couples: Exploring the Attraction." *Pastoral Psychology* 60.

Kim, Claire Jean. 1999. "The Racial Triangulation of Asian Americans." *Politics and Society* 27: 105–138.

Kim, Elaine. 1990. "'Such Opposite Creatures': Men and Women in Asian American Literature." *Michigan Quarterly Review* 29: 70.

Kitano, Harry R. L. 2004. *Asian Americans: Emerging Minorities*. New York: Prentice Hall.

Kohut, Andrew. 2012. "The Rise of Asian Americans." *Pew Research Center*.

LaVeist, Thomas. *Minority Populations and Health: An Introduction to Health Disparities in the United States*. San Francisco: Jossey-Bass, 2005.

Lee, Sharon, and Marilyn Fernandez. 1998. "Trends in Asian American Racial/Ethnic Intermarriage: A Comparison of 1980 and 1990 Census Data." *Sociological Perspectives* 41(2): 323–342.

Leopold, Todd, and Ashley Fantz. 2014. "Roommates, 'A Really Great Kid' among Victims." *CNN*. Archived from the original on May 30, 2014. Retrieved July 1, 2014. www.cnn.com/2014/05/25/us/santa-barbara-shooting-victims.

Lewis, A. E., M. Chesler, and T. A. Forman. 2000. "The Impact of 'Colorblind' Ideologies on Students of Color: Intergroup Relations at a Predominantly White University." *Journal of Negro Education* 74–91.

Ludden, Jennifer. 2014. "Student Activists Keep Pressure on Campus Sexual Assault." *NPR*. www.npr.org/2014/08/26/343352075/student-activists-keep-sexual-assault-issues-in-the-spotlight.

Margolis, Eric. 2001. *The Hidden Curriculum in Higher Education*. New York: Routledge.

"Meet Alexandra Wallace: The UCLA Ranting Racist." 2011. *Co-ed Magazine*. http://coedmagazine.com.

Meszaros, Julia. 2014. "Elliot Rodger and the Effeminization of Asian Men." *Huffington Post*. www.huffingtonpost.com/julia-meszaros/elliot-rodger-and-the-effeminization-of-asian-men_b_5401516.html.

Moore, Wendy L. 2008. *Reproducing Racism: White Space, Elite Law Schools, and Racial Inequality*. Lanham, MD: Rowman and Littlefield.

Office of Minority Health. 2011. "Health Status of Asian American and Pacific Islander Women." http://minorityhealth.hhs.gov.

Park, Julie. 2008. "Race and the Greek System in the 21st Century: Centering the Voices." *NASPA Journal* 45(1): 103–132.

Pascoe, C. J. 2007. *Dude, You're a Fag: Masculinity and Sexuality in High School*. Los Angeles: University of California Press.

Prashad, Vijay. 2001. "Genteel Racism." *Amerasia Journal* 26(3): 27–31.

Prasso, Sheridan. 2006. *The Asian Mystique: Dragon Ladies, Geisha Girls, and Our Fantasies of the Exotic Orient*. Cambridge, MA: Public Affairs.

Pyke, Karen D., and Denise L. Johnson. 2003. "Asian American Women and Racialized Femininities: 'Doing' Gender across Cultural Worlds." *Gender and Society* 17(1).

Ray, R., and J.A. Rosow. 2010. "Getting Off and Getting Intimate: How Normative Institutional Arrangements Structure Black and White Fraternity Men's Approaches toward Women." *Men and Masculinities* 12(5): 523–546.

Romero, Dennis. 2014. "Racist, Anti-Asian Flier Rocks UCLA, USC Campuses." *LA Blogs*. www.laweekly.com/informer/2014/02/11/racist-anti-asian-flier-rocks-ucla-usc-campuses.

Rosenbloom, S.R., and N. Way. 2004. "Experiences of Discrimination among African American, Asian American, and Latino Adolescents in an Urban High School." *Youth and Society* 35(4).

Rosenfeld, Michael. 2005. "A Critique of Exchange Theory in Mate Selection." *American Journal of Sociology* 110(5): 284–325.

Sassler, S., and K. Joyner. 2011. "Social Exchange and the Progression of Sexual Relationships in Emerging Adulthood." *Social Forces* 90(1): 223–245.

Schippers, Mimi. 2007. "Recovering the Feminine Other: Femininity, Masculinity, and Gender Hegemony." *Theory and Society* 36: 85–102.

Sidanius, Jim, Colette Van Laar, Shanna Levin, and Stacey Sinclair. 2004. "Ethnic Enclaves and the Dynamics of Social Identity on the College Campus: The Good, the Bad, and the Ugly." *Journal of Personality and Social Psychology* 87(1): 96–110.

Suck My Duke. 2007. "Calling All Crazies." *The Truth about Duke*. http://suckmyduke.blogspot.com.

Suh, Stephen. 2010. "The Korean Student Organization: Institutional Liberalism and the Ethnicity Based Student Group." Unpublished manuscript.

Takagi, Dana Y. 1993. "Asian Americans and Racial Politics: A Postmodern Paradox." *Social Justice* 20(1): 115–122.

Takaki, Ronald. 1998. *Strangers from a Different Shore*. Boston: Back Bay.

Tatum, Beverly Daniel. 1997. *"Why Are All the Black Kids Sitting Together in the Cafeteria?" And Other Conversations about Race*. New York: Basic.

Taylor, Paul. 2010. "Marrying Out." *Pew Research Center*.

Teranishi, Robert. 2010. *Asians in the Ivory Tower: Dilemmas of Racial Inequality in American Higher Education*. New York: Teachers College Press.

Tong, Benson. 1994. *Unsubmissive Women: Chinese Prostitutes in Nineteenth-Century San Francisco*. Norman: University of Oklahoma Press.

Tuan, Mia. 2003. *Forever Foreigners or Honorary Whites? The Asian Ethic Experience*. New Brunswick, NJ: Rutgers University Press.

US Census Bureau. 2004. "American Community Survey," Selected Population Profiles, S0201.

Van Dijk, Teun. 2000. "New(s) Racism: A Discourse Analytical Approach." In *Ethnic Minorities and the Media*, edited by S. Cottle, 33–49. Milton Keynes, UK: Open University Press.

Vera, Hernan, and Andrew M. Gordon. 2003. *Screen Saviors: Hollywood Fictions of Whiteness*. Lanham, MD: Rowman and Littlefield.

Wallace, Alexander. 2011. "Asians in the Library." www.youtube.com.

Wei, Johnny. 2013. "An Asian-American's Response to the Backlash against Kappa Sigma." *Duke Chronicle*. www.dukechronicle.com/articles/2013/02/07/asian-americans-response-backlash-against-kappa-sigma.

Wu, Frank. 2003. *Yellow: Race in America beyond Black and White*. New Haven, CT: Yale University Press.

Yang, Lin. 2011. "The Hard Part Is Getting In: Asian Americans Navigate the Racially Charged Politics of the College Admissions Process." *Hyphen*. www.hyphenmagazine.com/magazine.

Index

A

African American 22, 24, 27–28, 30, 36, 40, 44–45, 54, 59, 74, 92, 96, 101, 110–112
antimiscegenation 65
Asian accomplishment 6, 77
Asian American out-dating 45, 63,
Asian American sexual politics 41–42, 44, 56, 62
Asian American Sexual Politics vii, 56
Asian student organizations 41
"Asian upbringing" frame 72–76
assimilation 62–63, 83

B

bamboo ceiling 53, 83
Black Sexual Politics 10, 69
Bonilla-Silva, Eduardo ix–x, 6–8, 20, 67
Bourdieu, Pierre 66

C

Chou and Feagin 21, 24, 30, 46
cognitive dissonance 68
collective narrative 32, 47
Collins, Patricia Hill 10–11, 45, 69–70
color-blind discourse 5, 7–8, 15, 21, 43, 46, 58, 98
color-blind ideology 11, 71, 82–85, 104–105
color-blind preferences 62
color-blind racism 6–9, 36–38, 43, 56–57, 100–101
Connell and Messerschmidt 44, 68
controlling images 10–11, 23, 37, 45, 56–57, 69–70
counter-narratives 13, 69, 101, 106

D

dating viii, 13, 32, 34–36, 45, 53–54, 58, 62–64, 66, 71–72, 74, 76, 84–85, 89, 102
discursive strategy 46
double consciousness: Asian American males 11–12, 50, 57, 59; racial 11–12, 59, 64, 68–69, 71–72, 80, 88, 90
Duke University x, 41

E

economic privilege 53
emasculation 56
emotional management 10, 46, 68, 97, 99, 106
emotional work 25, 58, 99
the Eroticized Other 30, 47
exotification 10, 57, 70, 87
explicit color-blindness 85–86

F

fetishization 87–88

G

Global South 66
Gupta, Sanjay 83

H

hegemonic femininity 45, 67, 71
hegemonic masculinity 8–9, 21, 35, 39, 44, 48, 50, 52–53, 57, 64, 67, 71
hegemonic partying environment 78
hegemonic sexualities 9, 11–12, 67–68, 70–71, 74, 80, 86–87, 89–90, 103
heritage management 90, 105
hidden university curriculum 2, 33, 46
Historically White Colleges and Universities (HWCUs) 3–4, 12, 15, 20–21, 46, 57, 99, 106–107
historically white Greek life 77
honorary white 11–12, 36, 42, 70–71
honorary white privileges 12, 36, 71

I

Immigration Act of 1990 65
implicit color-blindness 85–86
intermarriage 63, 65
internalization 34–35, 62, 80–81
interracial relationships 10, 15, 56, 58, 61–62, 67–69, 86, 88
intersectionality 10–11, 42, 46, 69–70, 90

J

Jim Crow racism 6–8, 43

K

Kim, Claire Jean 43, 59

L

language capital 66, 81

M

media objectification 11, 23, 31, 50–52
media portrayals 57, 62
model minority vii, 5–7, 26, 30–31, 42, 46–47, 54, 63, 83–84, 103–104

N

normalized ideology 20, 22, 62

O

Orientalization 15, 62

P

Pacific Islander 13, 27, 38, 49, 96
partner selection 48, 55

people of color 8–9, 11, 20–22, 24, 26, 28–29, 33, 35, 37–38, 44, 54, 57, 61–62, 66, 69–70, 77–80, 88–89, 98–101, 104, 106–107
phallocentric masculinity 51
phenotypic capital 9–10, 66–68, 88, 104
post-Civil Rights era realities 7, 43

R

racial castration 15, 56, 62
racial discrimination 2, 8, 43, 62, 104–105
racial inequality 7–8, 12, 43
"racial middle" 42
racial romantic structure 54
racial segregation 6–7, 25, 29, 65
racial selectivity 85
racial self-hate 52
racial structure 2, 6, 8, 11, 20–21, 23, 26, 37, 43, 45, 58
racialization 25, 42
racialized love 45
racialized romantic preferences 46
"rape tolerant" cultures 48
"reverse-yellow fever" 86, 89
Rodger, Elliot 61–62
romantic relationships 34, 75

S

sexualized racism i, 15, 30–32, 36, 38, 43, 46–48, 57, 102
social exchange theory 64, 66–67, 86, 90
stereotypes 2, 4, 15, 22–23, 30, 33, 44, 47–48, 51, 54, 57, 81, 98, 107
stigma 23, 50, 57, 78, 98
submissiveness 48, 55

subordinated masculinities 9, 44, 67
subservience 55

T

tri-racial model 9, 11, 17, 44, 67, 70–71

U

University of California, Santa Barbara 61

W

war on women 61
war refugees 82
white habitus viii, 8–9, 11–12, 20–23, 25–26, 29–30, 32–33, 35–38, 46, 57, 64, 69, 71, 77, 79, 81–82, 85–87, 99, 105
white hegemonic beauty 66, 80
white hegemonic ideology 98
white hegemonic standards 80
white institutionalized space 21, 42, 58, 106
white privilege 6, 28, 30, 36, 45, 53, 62, 71, 77, 98, 104
white racial frame vii, 3–4, 6, 11, 21–22, 33, 35, 46, 52, 54, 57, 62, 66, 70, 72, 76, 78–79, 81–82, 99, 101, 107
white racial hierarchy 44
"white-washed" Asian Americans 33, 79

Y

"yellow fever" 48–50, 54–55, 86, 88–89
"yellow targeting" 86